The Archaeology of Race and Class at Timbuctoo

UNIVERSITY PRESS OF FLORIDA

Florida A&M University, Tallahassee
Florida Atlantic University, Boca Raton
Florida Gulf Coast University, Ft. Myers
Florida International University, Miami
Florida State University, Tallahassee
New College of Florida, Sarasota
University of Central Florida, Orlando
University of Florida, Gainesville
University of North Florida, Jacksonville
University of South Florida, Tampa
University of West Florida, Pensacola

THE ARCHAEOLOGY OF RACE AND CLASS AT TIMBUCTOO

A Black Community in New Jersey

CHRISTOPHER P. BARTON

Foreword by Guy Weston

University Press of Florida

Gainesville · Tallahassee · Tampa · Boca Raton

Pensacola · Orlando · Miami · Jacksonville · Ft. Myers · Sarasota

Publication of this work is made possible by a Sustaining the Humanities through the American Rescue Plan grant from the National Endowment for the Humanities.

27 26 25 24 23 22   6 5 4 3 2 1

Library of Congress Cataloging-in-Publication Data
Names: Barton, Christopher P., 1983– author. | Weston, Guy, author of
  foreword.
Title: The archaeology of race and class at Timbuctoo : a black community
  in New Jersey / Christopher P. Barton ; foreword by Guy Weston.
Description: Gainesville : University Press of Florida, [2022] | Includes
  bibliographical references and index.
Identifiers: LCCN 2021040773 (print) | LCCN 2021040774 (ebook) | ISBN
  9780813069272 (hardback) | ISBN 9780813070049 (pdf)
Subjects: LCSH: African Americans—New Jersey—History. | Excavations
  (Archaeology)—New Jersey. | Timbuctoo (N.J.)—History. | Timbuctoo
  (N.J.)—Antiquities. | BISAC: SOCIAL SCIENCE / Archaeology | SOCIAL
  SCIENCE / Anthropology / Cultural & Social
Classification: LCC E185.93.N54 B37 2022 (print) | LCC E185.93.N54
  (ebook) | DDC 974.9/610496073—dc23
LC record available at https://lccn.loc.gov/2021040773
LC ebook record available at https://lccn.loc.gov/2021040774

The University Press of Florida is the scholarly publishing agency for the State University System of Florida, comprising Florida A&M University, Florida Atlantic University, Florida Gulf Coast University, Florida International University, Florida State University, New College of Florida, University of Central Florida, University of Florida, University of North Florida, University of South Florida, and University of West Florida.

University Press of Florida
2046 NE Waldo Road
Suite 2100
Gainesville, FL 32609
http://upress.ufl.edu

To Dave Orr, who introduced me to Timbuctoo,
and to Mary Weston, who made me fall in love with it

CONTENTS

FIGURES

TABLES

FOREWORD

Timbuctoo means different things to different people. My first acquaintance with Timbuctoo came from my great-grandmother, who was born there in 1902. She and her siblings sometimes spoke of their youth in Timbuctoo, fondly known as "Bucktoe." To me, it was an unremarkable place where ancestors grew up. I had no idea they were the fourth generation to live there and I was clueless about any historic significance.

I later got some sense of its uniqueness through my own genealogy research, but I did not appreciate the extent to which Timbuctoo was a veritable goldmine of African American history and culture until 2009, when a group of anthropologists and historians proposed a research project in collaboration with our local government. They spoke of topics like archaeology, history, historic preservation, and community education. The history was fascinating. I learned that there were newspaper articles going back to at least the 1850s and records that verified land ownership, records of schools and churches, and other legal documents. But archaeology? When I hear the word archaeology, I think of places like Egypt or the Mayan ruins, but rural New Jersey? What did I know? It quickly became clear that a portion of my ancestors' homeland would become an archaeological site.

Community residents, including my young nieces and a nephew, learned how to dig and participated in the excavation. They found things like old bricks and pieces of pottery and glassware. I thought it was trash. The archaeologists said it was treasure because they provided insight into Timbuctoo's past. I learned that the types of bricks used to construct a home were predictive of the social class of the home builders and that other items indicated the material consumption of Timbuctoo residents. Mason jars and crops led to conclusions about canning practices and diet. Together, all these elements began to paint a picture of Timbuctoo's past that I did not think was possible, given the dearth of narratives left by early residents. Acting as key informants, Timbuctoo elders recounted recollections of their youth and family stories, oral histories that provided further insight into Timbuctoo.

There was even a political interpretation to these findings that pointed out how my ancestors and their neighbors did not have access to the same caliber of consumer goods as the region at large, how they made do with what they had, and how they persevered in spite of all the obstacles they faced in their pursuit of freedom and autonomy.

My chief mentor in much of this was a graduate student who was soon to become an archaeology professor by the name of Dr. Christopher Barton. I was excited to learn that Dr. Barton's extensive research and interpretation is available in this book. Dr. Barton's work begins to fill a substantial void in published work about antebellum African American people. I am very pleased to have learned so much from him and even happier that the information is now available for public consumption. He adds a political dimension to the narrative that's not widely appreciated. It is very timely, given recent developments in our society just this year.

Guy Weston
September 27, 2020

ACKNOWLEDGMENTS

Projects like this are never the result of one or even just a handful of people. They are the product of years of interaction with many people. I was first introduced to Timbuctoo by Dave Orr of Temple University. Dave's passion for archaeology and vision for the site excited me even before I visited that grassy meadow on top of a hill. When we finally visited, standing atop that hill with a smile that could light the darkest night was Mary Weston, a descendant of John Bruer (also spelled Brewer). Mary's love of everything and everyone, especially all things related to Timbuctoo, was infectious. Through the ups and downs of this project, Dave and Mary have been my rocks, providing me with support and love. They have made me into the person that I am today, and for that this book is dedicated to them.

Many thanks to the former residents and descendants who opened up their lives for the research that went into this project, especially Joseph Rogers Sr. You are greatly missed.

I am thankful to the Timbuctoo Discovery Project, especially Paul Schopp and Marylin Phifer. I especially thank Guy Weston for his friendship and support over the years. Guy is a brilliant historian and a passionate defender of Timbuctoo. A portion of this project was supported by a grant from Westampton Township thanks to the guidance of Mayors Carolyn Chang and Sidney Camp. Additional funding was provided by a Winterthur Museum Garden and Library fellowship.

Over the years I have received support from a number of senior scholars, including Stacey Camp, Jim Delle, Cheryl LaRoche, Chris Matthews, Carol McDavid, Paul Mullins, Charles Orser, and countless others. I am also indebted to Rich Veit, who has been a great source of knowledge and a great friend. Paul Garrett provided an outside perspective to this project that helped me push the boundaries of my interpretation beyond archaeology. Michael Stewart is one of the hardest working professionals I know; his knowledge continues to inspire junior archaeologists. Patricia Markert's brilliance helped me in every phase of this project. Trish represents the future of our field; she will push the limits of our discipline. I am also indebted to my dear friend and editor at large, Kyle Somerville, who over the years has read and reviewed countless drafts of my work. He has been a true friend when I've needed one the most.

*   *   *

Thanks also to my family, Mom, Jamie, Katie, and Dad, may he rest in power. None of this could have been done without the support of my loving wife, Jess. When I was told that college wasn't for me, she gave me the support and love I needed to push through. I thank her for all the late nights and early mornings that she had to listen to my Timbuctoo ramblings. She is and will always be my love.

*   *   *

Finally, to my son, Asher, you are my world.

INTRODUCTION

This is not my story. Stories of resistance, perseverance, and triumph echo only in the hearts and minds of the descendants of Timbuctoo, New Jersey. My ancestors did not feel the shackles of slavery, my family did not taste the bitterness of segregation, and we do not endure the gazes of modern racism.

I am an archaeologist; I do not own the past. The fact that I know how to excavate and how to make sense out of thousands of artifacts does not give me the sole right to interpret the past. We archaeologists are not the only tellers of history. We are not the lone gatekeepers of the past. We are but a fraction of the broader community that also finds meaning and significance in such sites. Timbuctoo is not my past, I am just a guy who was lucky enough to dig there.

Timbuctoo was founded in 1826, when Hezekiah Hall and brothers David, Ezekiel, and Wardell Parker purchased individual lots totaling 4.4 acres from William Hilyard, a local white Quaker. Hall and the Parkers are all believed to be runaway captives from Maryland (Weston 2018). The bold steps they and other residents took to secure their freedom and to ensure that their families would not have to endure enslavement are at the core of the history of Timbuctoo. Timbuctoo means a lot to a lot of different people; to some it is home, to others it is a metaphor for America's story of race and class. For me, at first, it was just a research topic. In 2009, I was introduced to Timbuctoo by Dave Orr, an archaeologist at Temple University who had spent much of his career working for the National Park Service. In the mid-1980s, Dave was invited to visit Timbuctoo to assess its archaeological potential. He argued that the site had potential but was unable to find funding to investigate it (figure 1.1, figure 1.2).

Figure 1.1. Map of New Jersey with a star indicating the location of Timbuctoo, Westampton, Burlington County. Source: Google Earth.

Figure 1.2. Historically, the core of Timbuctoo has been identified as the roughly 50 acres between
Rancocas Road (north), Rancocas Creek (south), Church Street (east), and Blue Jay Hill Road
(west). Source: Google Earth.

In 1999, Catherine Turton of the National Park Service began to gather historic documents related to the site, including deeds, probate records, census records, newspaper articles, and birth and death notices (Turton 1999). Turton compiled her work and gave it to Westampton Township officials, the town in which Timbuctoo is located. Then, in 2004, Westampton Township acquired four of the roughly 50 acres of what once was Timbuctoo. In 2007, Mayor Sidney Camp contacted Orr to discuss the potential for archaeological work at the site. Orr suggested that William Chadwick and Peter Leach (2009) of John Milner Associates, Inc. be contracted to complete a noninvasive geophysical survey of the four acres that included the use of ground-penetrating radar and magnetometry (figure 1.3).

In 2009, a group of descendants, interested community members, scholars, and professionals came together to form the Timbuctoo Discovery Project, now known as the Timbuctoo Advisory Committee. The committee is chaired by Guy Weston, a descendant of John Bruer (also spelled Brewer), who settled in Timbuctoo in 1829. The committee's purpose is to advise the township, the local land development board, and all municipal agencies on any issues related to the history and archaeology of Timbuctoo, as stated in Westampton Township Ordinance 6-2015 (Township of Westampton 2015). The committee also offers public outreach and educational programs, including Timbuctoo Day, an event that includes speakers, reenactors, and exhibits that relate to the community and to Black history.

From the outset of my introduction to the committee, we established that any and all work pertaining to the archaeology—planning, research, excavating, processing artifacts, interpreting, and disseminating archaeological work—would operate through a fully collaborative, pragmatic framework. Degrees of community participation vary in archaeology, from projects where members of the public are spectators during excavation to the full incorporation of stakeholders in every phase of the archaeological process. Before I came to know Timbuctoo, I had worked at a site as a graduate student that took a very "velvet rope" approach to all archaeology, to the point where the public was escorted off the premises and kept 200 feet away from all excavation. While there are situations and sites that require such a hands-off approach, this specific case made me question my role as an archaeologist and archaeology's responsibility to the community. Thus, when I got to Timbuctoo I was determined to make all aspects of the archaeological process open to stakeholders as collaborators (Barton and Markert 2012).

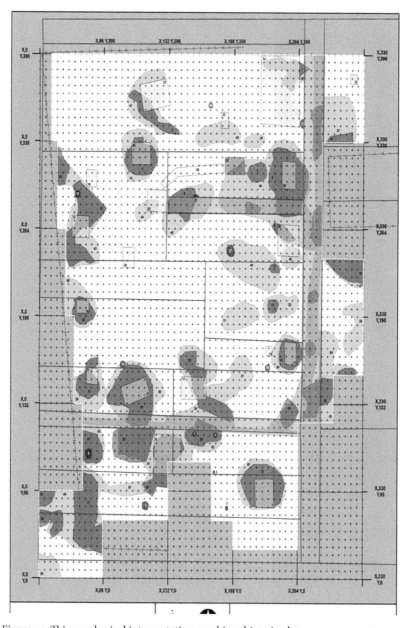

Figure 1.3. This geophysical interpretation combines historic plot maps, a magnetometer survey, and a ground-penetrating radar survey of the four acres of Timbuctoo that was held by Westampton Township during fieldwork. The seventeen shaded squares represent possible house or outbuilding foundations. The three medium-shaded rectangles represent historic pathways, including what once was Haywood Street to the east. Created by William Chadwick. Source: Chadwick and Leach 2009.

Edward González-Tennant (2014) identifies two frameworks for community-engaged archaeology. First is participatory archaeology, which he defines as the production of knowledge by archaeologists with limited involvement of community members and other stakeholders. In participatory archaeology, stakeholders participate only in the laborious aspects of fieldwork—for example, in excavation and/or laboratory work—but are not involved in the other processes of archaeology, such as interpreting artifacts and disseminating knowledge. This framework is widely used in archaeology and many continue to see it as the definitive form of public archaeology. But González-Tennant offers a second framework—collaborative archaeology. Here, a group of collaborators that includes archaeologists and stakeholders develop an environment for exploring the past through equal partnerships. Archaeologists have rarely been willing to fully integrate community members as equal partners because we have balked at giving up or sharing power. The collaboration continuum spans from outreach programs that seek to educate the public about archaeological projects to complex projects in which various stakeholders are equal partners in the planning, excavation, interpretation, and dissemination of archaeology. Numerous programs operate along this continuum, but here I focus on three projects that influenced me in my study of collaborative historical archaeology.

First is Mark Leone's work in Annapolis, Maryland. Leone was interested in the role ideologies played in the interpretation of Annapolis. He argued that despite the city's racial diversity, limited information was presented to the public regarding Black history. Leone argued that racial ideologies were used illusionary, social constructions used to mask the real social and economic similarities between marginalized communities. Leone contended that if archaeologists interacted with the public, we could assess what people's beliefs were and challenge them through education. This critical theory approach involved limited collaboration between archaeologists, the public, and stakeholders and much of the power to interpret the past rested with the archaeologists. Leone feared that the knowledge generated could be hijacked to promote a whitewashed narrative of historical progress and deliberately withheld power. He and other critical theorists (Wurst and Fitts 1999; McGuire 2008) operated as the vanguards between the archaeology they uncovered and the information they presented to the public. This means that in nearly every step of the archaeological process, a select few professionals plan, analyze, and interpret for the broader community. While Leone did consult with stakeholders, especially Black community members of Annapolis, he used a top-down approach for all of the planning, excavation, interpretation, and dissemination of the work.

In truth, in the early stages of our work at Timbuctoo, our project followed a similar model. Some members of the committee did not see the value of partnering with people who were not scholars and did not believe that knowledge produced by stakeholders was equal to the knowledge of professionals. Discussions and disagreements are part of every archaeological process, but when committee members do not value the unique experiences, meanings, and insights of others, collaboration fails. Every archaeological project has shortcomings or things that in hindsight we wish that we had done differently. I regret that I did not fight hard enough to incorporate a truly collaborative framework in the early years at Timbuctoo because I was a young archaeologist who was too intimidated by some members of the committee who challenged pragmatism and threatened my future career. But every obstacle that hinders us can also be used as a self-reflective lesson to strength ourselves and our projects. I spent many restless nights, tossing and turning over our work at Timbuctoo and in the end it was the descendants, particularly, the Westons, who supported and uplifted by spirits in trying times.

The second project that operated along this continuum of collaboration and has been influential in the field of African Diaspora archaeology is the African Burial Ground in New York City. In 1991, crews working on the construction of a 34-story office building for the United States General Services Administration (GSA) uncovered the first remains of what would be over 400 individuals. The property was referred to as the Negroes Burying Ground on historical maps and was used from circa 1712 to 1794. Similar to many other Black cemeteries (Davidson 2007; Barton 2021; LaRoche 2014), the African Burial Ground was largely forgotten and over time the property was redeveloped and partially used as a landfill. Fearing rising development costs, the GSA sought to continue construction and exhume remains. This created a controversy in the Black communities of New York, as the GSA had not consulted them in the planning of the site. After much debate and protests, the GSA brought in Michael Blakey of Howard University. Given the sensitive issues associated with excavating and analyzing human remains, the Black communities of New York were not able to collaborate, but they did become partners in determining the future of the African Burial Ground as a National Historic Landmark and National Monument. However, as LaRoche and Blakey (1997, 97) state, "The struggle for control of the African Burial Ground site was a struggle to have the voice of the community heeded. Exclusion of the direct community involvement as the project progresses removes ethical, moral, spiritual, and social issues and obligations from community control." Despite the critical missteps the GSA made in the early stages of the project, the Black communities were able to participate in the future direction of the African Burial Ground, in large part thanks to the work of Cheryl LaRoche and other anthropologists (LaRoche and Blakey 1997).

The third project that has incorporated collaboration and has been influential for the archaeology at Timbuctoo is Carol McDavid's (2002, 2007) work at the Levi Jordan Plantation in Brazoria, Texas. The plantation was established in 1848 and has been the focus of archaeological research since the 1990s. McDavid did not work on the excavation of the plantation; she focused on collaborating with descendant communities of both the enslaved and the enslavers to interpret the archaeological findings. For McDavid, collaboration in archaeology is a fully pragmatic act that values every participant equally for their insights and contributions to the project. Following the work of Rorty (1991), pragmatists contend that human interactions can be thought of as "a historically situated, contingent, pluralistic *conversation*" (McDavid 2002, 305). For archaeologists, McDavid challenges the essentialist perspectives that reduce history to a single narrative. She argues that "while pragmatists do *not* believe that one truth is as good as another, they do believe that humans can and will be able to discover, over time, which truths are more meaningful and useful" (McDavid 2000, 305). The way for archaeologists to uncover these more meaningful truths is through pluralistic conversations with diverse stakeholders. McDavid calls for archaeologists to reflect on how our research serves and disserves the stakeholders of a community. The creation of a website (webarchaeology.com) was central to her work. It brought together all of the various voices and interpretations of the communities. In contrast to the top-down-framework approach to community archaeology Mark Leone used in the Archaeology in Annapolis project, McDavid's work seeks to include *everyone*'s voice in the conversations about the past as a way of creating more holistic, inclusive representations.

This approach has drawn criticism for two reasons. First is the fear among archaeologists that it gives away their power to interpret the past. I remember being criticized by senior scholars for collaborating with the public and stakeholders. They were concerned that I would lose my "objectivity" if I worked with people for whom these sites had meaning, that I would lose my role as a "neutral scientist" if our interpretations were generated through collaboration. Senior archaeologists asked me, "What if you found something that the community didn't like? Would they alter your interpretations? If people outside the field have influence, how will this affect your writing?" My answers to these questions focused on the reality that no archaeological site belongs to an archaeologist. If the people for whom Timbuctoo meant so much didn't like something that was uncovered, we would work to find common ground. We archaeologists do not lose our power as trained professionals when we collaborate; instead, our role transitions from "gatekeepers" to partners with communities affected by our work. Our knowledge about research, excavation, and analysis constitutes a unique set of skills that others do not have, but that knowledge does not make us the only people with invaluable skills that can be used in uncovering meaning in the past. In a community-engaged collaboration, the power of the archaeologist is still there, it is just that the experiences of stakeholders add new levels of meaning and significance. Pragmatic archaeology means that each person connected to a site has a voice in the pluralistic conversations of the past. The archaeologist's voice has power to inform the ways that a site is excavated or analyzed but their voice does not drown out the voices of stakeholders. Pragmatism means not talking *at* people but talking *with* people about the past.

When only one person analyzes the past, it can limit the potential for an accurate portrayal. Not everyone experiences and interprets the past in the same way. People in the past witnessed many things differently from each other and differently from how we in the present see those things. While objective facts can be identified, the interpretation of the archaeological record is not a straightforward practice. As responsible scientists, archaeologists must use as much evidence as possible to uncover the meanings inscribed in the archaeological record. This means including stakeholders as equal partners in this discovery is needed for moral and ethical reasons, but also, doing so simply ensures that we are being good scientists.

A fully collaborative project calls for all stakeholders to be included in the archaeological process. This relates to the second fear regarding a pragmatic approach, that too many voices can muffle the voices of descendants, residents, or people who have intimate connections to a site (McGuire 2008, 7). The argument is that if we include all voices, even fringe groups or individuals, then the meaning and/or interpretations of sites can be hijacked and the truth claims of stakeholders can be lost. McGuire (2009, 60–61) argues that including too many voices in a collaborative framework can have the opposite of the desired effect of unmasking systems of repression.

He contends that when the voices of everyone, even those of people with outlandish theories, like the idea that pyramids were built by aliens, are seen as equal to those of archaeologists and stakeholders, the narratives developed in collaboration can themselves become repressive.

For example, in the authorized public memory (Delle 2008; Barton and Markert 2012) of New Jersey, the role of Quakers in the Underground Railroad is often exaggerated and the reality that the network to freedom was operated predominantly by Black individuals and groups is downplayed (McDaniel and Julye 2009; LaRoche 2014). Authorized public memory is defined as the narratives recognized "authorities" (historians, archaeologists, museum professionals, historic interpreters, and scholars) often use to celebrate or commemorate something in the past (Delle 2008, 65–66). Scholars, museums, and institutions use authorized public memories to shape the narrative of the past for the benefit of those in power in the present. The result is that authorized public memories often represent the past as monolithic in order to construct a collective identity among varying social groups. McDaniel and Julye argue that the authorized public memory that Quakers influenced the Underground Railroad is based on several factors. First, Quakers had the reputation of being abolitionists because of the early stance the Society of Friends took against enslavement. However, McDaniel and Julye (2009, 97) note that Quakers' active participation in the Underground Railroad was not greater than that of other denominations. Second, the fact that Philadelphia, which had a sizable Quaker population, was the closest city north of the Mason-Dixon line meant that many people escaping slavery spent some time there. This activity in the city created the oversimplified misconception that Quakers were the operators of the Underground Railroad. Thirdly, McDaniel and Julye (2009, 98) argue that the popularity of Harriet Beecher Stowe's *Uncle Tom's Cabin,* in which the white Quaker couple, the Hallidays, gave refuge to escapees George and Eliza, furthered the misrepresentation through popular culture that Quakers were active in the network to freedom. Although *some* Quakers were active participants in the Underground Railroad, most individuals were ambivalent about helping escapees (McDaniel and Julye 2009, 97). However, the actions of the few Quakers and the reasons argued by McDaniel and Julye have whitewashed the authorized public memory of the Underground Railroad.

Even more often, as we see at Timbuctoo, authorized public memories generalize about or ignore difficult histories. When such histories are part of the memories of living people, authorized public memories regard those lived experiences as distant events with no connection to the present. This disconnect between the past and the present creates the narrative that we have progressed, that the injustice that happened in the past does not still trouble us today. An example of this at Timbuctoo was that when a multi-vocal framework was developing, the only topic some people were interested in was the authorized public memory about the role of Quakers in the formation of the community. If the project had focused only on these voices, we would have continued to whitewash the history of Timbuctoo and neglected the agency of Black people in resisting slavery. We had to redirect our approach to ensure that the voices of archaeologists, descendants, and stakeholders were taken into greater consideration than those that sought to reproduce the authorized public memories of Timbuctoo.

The counterargument to the practice of emphasizing some voices over others asks Who are the ones who select the voices (McDavid 2002)? This is an important question because if we try to silence some voices, we run the risk of muting the voices that we seek to amplify in collaboration. McDavid cautions that when archaeologists select some voices, their interpretations of the past could be inaccurate and that some archaeologists could engage in the repression and marginalization that we seek to expose. Instead, she argues that we need to include *all* voices in collaboration, no matter how fringe they may seem, and that through discourse we will eventually be able to develop more holistic interpretations of the past without the risk of alienating or marginalizing anyone.

While I agree with the sentiment of this truly pragmatic approach, I am wary of including every voice in a discourse on a site like Timbuctoo, given the history of Black disenfranchisement and the threat that the voices of some misinformed individuals who argued that New Jersey was a state characterized by racial harmony would be equally weighted against those of descendants. For example, in 2010, I gave a presentation to the Burlington County Board of Freeholders that discussed issues of race relations at Timbuctoo and a confrontation between Timbuctoo residents and the Ku Klux Klan in the 1950s. After the presentation an audience member, a local white woman, approached me and stated that the Klan was never in Burlington County and that I was simply a "race baiter" who was trying to stir up tensions. The sad irony is that she made her false argument during a week when the Ku Klux Klan had been dropping off newsletters on residents' doorsteps in nearby Shamong (Barton and Markert 2012). During our brief conversation, it was clear that the woman had no intention of creating an open dialogue. She simply wanted to promote the authorized public memory of racial harmony in the region. Our fear was that if we included similar people in our collaboration, the project would run the risk of marginalizing stakeholders such as descendants and former residents. Doing so would make us complicit in the continued whitewashing of the past. Simply put, some voices in the collaborative process should be elevated over others. The voices of descendant communities and former residents for whom the sites hold a deep-seated connection should be amplified through our archaeology work, not muffled by the screams of the misguided.

That being said, it is not my place to unilaterally accept or reject potential voices. As a committee member, it is my role to listen and share what knowledge and/or advice I can offer. While this framework could restrict broader participation, my fear is that too many varying voices, including potentially damaging ones, could lead to the silencing of voices that have been marginalized. Also, community-engaged, collaborative archaeology is not easy. It is hard to get people to meet, exchange ideas, and then follow up on agreed-upon actions. One of my concerns about including too many voices is that it can lead to disarray or—even worse—the end of a project. But if we select some voices over others, who are the ones who select those voices? This is not an easy question to answer, and I would contend that it is never the archaeologist's role to select voices. Instead, it should be left to the community. At Timbuctoo, that includes descendants, residents, and Westampton Township officials. I use Sonya Atalay's (2012, 90) definition of community as "a unit of identity that is reinforced through social interactions and characterized by a degree of common identity, shared experiences, and/or geographic proximity." Experiences can be shaped by class, ethnicity, gender, location, race, and religion and often intersect with one another to further deepen collective identity within the community. Communities are diverse in terms of membership and identities, and their physical and cultural boundaries can be both well defined and fluid (Atalay 2012, 91). A pragmatic archaeology that includes community voices as equal partners in research makes for both a more democratic archaeology and a more holistic interpretation of the past. As social scientists, archaeologists want every piece of evidence to research and hypothesize about a site. The inclusion of community voices not only adds more evidence to bolster our research, it also provides diverse perspectives that contribute to a fuller portrayal of history. It is simply good, ethical science to democratize archaeology. But our work should not stop at democratizing archaeology as a way of studying the past; we must also act collectively to make the world a more humane place. Collective action is the behavior of a community of individuals with shared experiences and interests (Saitta 2007, 5). These communities' collective actions can be directed toward a common goal or goals. In the case of Timbuctoo, two of the goals were to use our collective action to help society think critically about the past and to use archaeology as social activism.

Archaeology and Social Activism

Critical theorists use knowledge of the past to create action in the present. The idea that theory, study, and present-day action are connected is drawn from Marxist theory. In archaeology, Randall McGuire has been on the forefront of using critical theory to promote political activism through praxis. Praxis is our ability to create change in society and in ourselves through informed action (McGuire 2008, 3). We study topics, excavate sites, and research people not for the sake of the past. We do these things so we can make informed decisions that will help us emancipate ourselves from repression in the present. McGuire (2009, 7–8) argues that praxis can come about only through collaboration (McGuire 2008, 7–8). At Timbuctoo, we used the approach of collaborative praxis to study how the past and the present are interconnected. Our archaeological and historical work focused on these connections with an emphasis on ideologies of race, class, and gender. Unfortunately, our efforts to use archaeology at Timbuctoo as a vehicle for social activism were greatly hampered by several factors. One was that I was a junior scholar who was trying to complete this early research within a rigid university system. Another was that some of the more conservative members of the Timbuctoo committee had contempt for social justice issues. They felt that the history of the site should be apolitical. They wanted our work to focus solely on Timbuctoo as a station along the Underground Railroad and on the roles that local white Quakers played in the founding of the community. While there is undoubted merit in researching this topic, it also limits our focus and fails to convey the whole history of Timbuctoo. In the end, our best attempts at using our praxis came from our presentations at local organizations, historical societies, and on Timbuctoo Day that openly discussed how the past is connected to present-day issues of social justice. Thankfully, during our fieldwork at Timbuctoo, the mayors—first Mayor Sidney Camp and then Mayor Carolyn Chang—were Democrats who wanted to both protect and preserve the site and connect its history to the present.

Both mayors were African Americans who were concerned about why a site with a rich history such as Timbuctoo was not included in the local authorized public memories of the area. For many of us on the Timbuctoo Discovery Project committee, this lack of public knowledge of the site was emblematic of the deeper issue of the failure to discuss Black history in New Jersey. Moreover, when our project at Timbuctoo began to garner attention, the focus of the public and the media was primarily the community's role in the Underground Railroad. Interest in the more recent past was limited. The more conservative members of the Timbuctoo committee shared this myopic focus.

Another fruitful avenue for using archaeology as social activism came through our open policy regarding volunteers. Children as young as 6 and adults over 80 collaborated in the archaeological process and discussed their life experiences. We found that creating a safe, open forum for dialogue in the field, in the laboratory, and in meeting rooms helped foster discussion that used our theories and our work to create action. The most enjoyable aspect of this action for me was when Mary Weston, a descendant and current resident of Timbuctoo, and I engaged with local Westampton students in talking about our work and about how modern issues of racism and sexism are rooted in the past. Weston, who resides in Timbuctoo, is Guy Weston's mother. She served as the first chair of the Timbuctoo committee. At our presentations, Weston and I would introduce ourselves, then I would ask the students "What is archaeology?" Then Weston and I would discuss Timbuctoo. I would talk about the archaeology and Weston would delve into the history and its connections to the present day. One of the connections that we would address is how race is a flawed social construct and how it influences the ways we see each other today. (Elsewhere I have written about the relationships between toys and ideologies of gender and race; see Barton and Somerville 2012, 2016; Barton 2021.) During our presentations, I would pass out boxes that I had filled with modern toys (plastic soldiers, a doll, one pink and one blue ball, etc.) and I would ask the children to tell me a story about who the boxes belonged to. I would say, "What type of toys are in the boxes? Tell me what you think about the person who owned these toys. What was their age/gender/class?" to try and elicit some interpretations from the children. I would try to steer the conversation toward questions about how gender is associated with toys. Our hope was that through this engagement, the children would begin to think differently about themselves and their interactions with others.

While this form of archaeology as social activism is not "radical" by any measure, trying to make the world a more humane place does not always call for radical action. Elsewhere (Barton 2021) I have argued that there is no one way to use our craft as social activism, that there is no how-to guide and there should not be a single manual. Social activism is a process and not a uniform product. Archaeology as social activism is very much a trial-and-error process in which you will likely have more failures than successes. This was the case for me at Timbuctoo, where I had hoped to use praxis through social activism but was unable to directly alter the authorized public memory that New Jersey was progressive toward Black peoples. But what is archaeology as social activism?

I believe that in some way, all archaeology is a form of social activism. All of us try to use our studies of the past to inform people in the present with the hopes of making the future better. By using our knowledge and theories to create positive action in the world, we are all using our craft for social activism. This may seem like a copout for some readers who want their socially engaged archaeology to be fiery and radical, but sometimes the most impactful collective action is not so overt. Many of us cannot be as activist in our projects as we would like because of where we work, the structure of our projects, and/or how we are funded. That was the case for me as a young archaeologist at Timbuctoo. But social activism through archaeology does not need to stop when the field season is done or the site report is completed. In many ways, this book in my own self-reflective attempt to make amends for my shortcomings in the past by discussing not only the history and archaeology at Timbuctoo but how we can use our knowledge of the past as praxis to create a better world.

Research Design

This book attempts to understand the historical and archaeological records of Timbuctoo. Like other archaeologists (Battle-Baptiste 2010; Davidson et al. 2006; Singleton 1999) who specialize in the African Diaspora, my first interest at Timbuctoo was to uncover cultural continuities in the archaeological record that could be traced back to West African cultural practices, but as we began to engage more with the historical and archaeological evidence, my research interests transitioned to trying to understand how the impoverished Black residents used their experiences, landscapes, and consumer power to improvise in their everyday lives. These became the guiding research questions for the project:

What were the social and economic statuses of the Timbuctoo
residents?

What access did the residents have to consumer goods and how did
structures of race, gender, age, and legal status affect their access
to goods?

What similarities and differences existed between Timbuctoo and
other Black communities in the region?

These research questions were part of this project early on. They were developed in collaboration with the Timbuctoo committee and thus reflect the interests of multiple parties. However, any shortcomings of this book are my own failures and in no way reflect poorly on the various stakeholders.

This book focuses on how the people of Timbuctoo used consumer culture, their landscape, and their resourcefulness to resist marginalizing structures of race and class. I had been mulling over this approach for some time as I tried to describe what I believe was represented in the archaeology at Timbuctoo when we hosted a local church group at the site on a hot summer day. At that meeting, as we stood in a circle and held hands with each other during prayer, the preacher praised the "poor" people of Timbuctoo and their ability to "stretch the soup with some water." I was unfamiliar with this turn of phrase, so I asked the preacher what it meant. She replied that Black people have endured so much and yet they have been able to persevere and make what they can out of this world. Stretching the soup with a little bit of water means drawing from a learned tradition of "making do" or improvising (Barton 2013). Drawing on the works of anthropologists (Stack 2008; Goode and Maskovsky 2002; Scheper-Hughes 1992) and archaeologists (Orser 1988, 2004; Matthews 2012, 2020), I interpret the archaeology of Timbuctoo as a reflection of how individuals socialized themselves to a habitus that negotiates racism and poverty.

Layout of the Book

Chapter 2 touches on the formation of racial structures in the United States and their connections to social and economic class. I then discuss how a lack of economic and social capital due to structures of race fostered a habitus that contested poverty. I draw from the works of Bourdieu (1977, 1984, 1986, 1990), Giddens (1979, 1991), and Ortner (1996, 1999, 2001) to talk about the relationships between social structures, practice, and habitus.

This chapter helps establish the theoretical framework for discussing the archaeological fieldwork at Timbuctoo.

In chapter 3, I discuss the history of Timbuctoo. The village was one of several other nineteenth-century free Black communities located throughout southern New Jersey. From Timbuctoo's founding in 1826, the community was a terminus along the Greenwich line of the Underground Railroad. Due to this active role in resisting slavery, the community was the target for slave catchers and their spies in the years leading up to the Civil War. I also discuss the military service of several of the residents in the United States Colored Troops for the Union Army and their return to Timbuctoo after the war. The community population declined in the latter half of the nineteenth century, as there was no longer a need to live together to create protections from slavery and residents looked for better economic opportunities elsewhere. However, a Black community remained at Timbuctoo that grew and declined over the years. By the 1960s–1970s, the size of the community had decreased to only a few households. By the early 2000s, the only aboveground features of the nineteenth-century community were gravestones in the cemetery. This chapter concludes with a discussion of the recent history of Timbuctoo and the archaeology of the Davis site.

This book takes a multiscalar approach to the archaeology of Timbuctoo. In chapter 4, I discuss the settlement pattern of the community, detailing how the layout may have connections to West Africa and to communal identity and protection. I focus on the Davis site and an interpretation of yard sweeping. Swept yards have a deep cultural connection to West African belief systems. They also had the functional purpose of creating an extension of the household for vocational and social activities. I discuss how landscapes both reflect and reconstruct intersecting identities of race and class.

Chapter 5 looks at interpretations of the building architecture of the Davis site drawing on examples from contemporaneous Black settlements. I also discuss the bricks of the foundation through the lens of experimental archaeology to underscore the resourcefulness of the occupants of the Davis site and of Timbuctoo residents. Through these interpretations of building materials and architecture we are better able to understand habitus and practice at Timbuctoo.

In chapter 6, I look at how Black residents of Timbuctoo interacted with consumerism in savvy ways, focusing on foodways. I discuss how people used home canning and the consumption of processed food to save time, energy, and money. I use the rise of peanut butter to national prominence as an example of how impoverished consumers used commodified foods. These interpretations are put in the contexts of World War I, the Great Depression, and World War II to emphasize the effects of national and global events on everyday practice at Timbuctoo.

In chapter 7, I complicate the narratives at Timbuctoo by discussing how even though poverty was a continuing theme at Timbuctoo, the people there were part of a developing consumer culture that promoted a genteel identity of belonging through consumption and display. Bric-a-brac artifacts recovered from the trash midden are examples of this construction of middle-class identity. However, residents used display through consumption not only to convey that they aspired to join the middle class; impoverished individuals also used display to fulfill their own desires. Even though many of the residents were on the lower end of the economic spectrum, they were a part of a larger social network that encouraged consumer desire, and they attempted to contest the negative label of "poor" through consumption and display.

A comparison of the histories and archaeologies of Timbuctoo with the Black New Jersey communities of Skunk Hollow (Geismar 1982) and Saddlertown is covered in chapter 8. I use these regional and national approaches to understand how the histories and archaeology of Timbuctoo are similar to what people experienced at other Black sites.

Structural marginalization is not limited to Black sites of the past. Communities of color still endure it today. This book concludes by arguing that the archaeology of Timbuctoo, like many other sites associated with repressed communities, should be used to connect our studies of the past to present-day issues of social justice. By using archaeology as social activism, we hope to not only make the field more relevant in the twenty-first century but to use our power as archaeologists to make a better, more humane world.

THE INTERSECTIONALITY
OF RACE AND CLASS

What we understand as race—the perception that there are different groups of people based on cultural and phenotypic traits—was developed during the Enlightenment (Orser 2004). However, people have been using phenotypes to create identities since before Egyptian hieroglyphics were used (Kelly 1991, 77). For example, in 440 BCE, Herodotus argued that the different characteristics of Egyptians' and Persians' skulls were influenced by cultural and environment. Going back even farther, we see depictions of what we would call people of different "races" in bas-reliefs in the Late Period of Egypt (664 to 332 BCE). While ancient people saw the spectrum of physical variations in humans, the ideology that biological race created these differences did not exist in the sense that we see it today in ancient times (Mertz 2008, 18–19).

In the seventeenth century, the pursuit of order in the natural and social worlds led to the development of racialist categories that were widely internalized and reproduced as a reality of our species (Epperson 1994, 1999). These perceived racial differences fostered an ideology that phenotypic diversity was evidence for human subspeciation. Some people even believed that the different races were different species (Smedley 1999, 174). The belief that unchanging categories of humans exist based on cultural and biological similarities and that some categories of humans are clearly different from other races is referred to as racialism (Echo-Hawk and Zimmerman 2006, 471; Roediger 2019). Racialism continues to be internalized and to be seen as the natural state of our species. For example, we are asked to provide information about our "race" to the US Census Bureau and to potential employers. Medical professionals treat Black patients differently than they do white patients. In a survey of medical students, Hoffman et al. (2016, 4298) found that 40 percent of first- and second-year white students believed that the skin of Black people is thicker than that of white people and that 78 percent of second-year students believed that the bones of Black people are denser and stronger than those of white people. These racialist beliefs among medical students result in real, and racist, disparities in how they assess the pain of Black patients and in inadequate treatment (4300).

Racialist beliefs affect how archaeologists practice their craft. Roger Echo-Hawk and Larry Zimmerman (2006, 476–477) point out that the use of craniometrics to identify racial affiliation is a common practice in archaeology that upholds racialism. They argue that

> archaeological racialism is damaging to archaeology and to the people archaeology studies because race distorts our understanding of humankind and human history. This outcome seriously undermines the ability of archaeology to contribute meaningfully to the ongoing construction of race in American culture.

They also state that "when American archaeologists claim to study such artifacts of racial culture as 'Native American prehistory' or 'African American history,' they are purveyors of racialism." This book in itself continues the tradition in archaeology of promoting the "warped status-quo" of race (Echo-Hawk and Zimmerman 2006, 462), in that its focus is the study of race within a Black community. However, given that 33.8 percent of Americans still believe that biology solely determines a person's racial identity" (Tillery 2018), we must continue to walk this tightrope to expunge the ideology of racialism while also showing how race influences daily life as a social construction. We are not at a point yet in our field or in our society where we can abandon studies of racial culture because racialization is part of our socialization from birth.

The perception that race is the natural state of humans is similar to Bourdieu's (1977) concept of doxa, which refers to all that a society takes for granted, or a belief that the "natural and social worlds" are "self-evident" (Bourdieu 1990, 164). In Western society, race is viewed as an objective, commonsense way of considering human variation that is still largely unchallenged. Race as doxa also continues the belief that there have always been different groups of people based on their physical traits and that there will always be different races.

However, race is not an objective, universally understood concept. It is subjective, and the traits used to place people in categories vary based on societies and individuals. One exercise I like to do with my students is to ask them to name the different human races. There are usually a few that everyone agrees about, but then the discussion often goes awry. I like to say, "What about the Irish race?" in response to which I get awkward stares and comments. Most of my students, and indeed many Americans, do not know that during the nineteenth century, Anglo-Americans did not consider Irish people to be white. In fact, their transformation to "whiteness" did not fully occur until the early twentieth century, after many Irish individuals and their descendants had become prominent political and business leaders. Moreover, the admission of the Irish into the white race was bolstered by Irish people's racist views that they were superior to people of color (Ignatiev 1995; Orser 2007, 110; Roediger 1991). The point of the discussion with my students is to show that even in the classroom, the subjectivity of race can vary between people from the same area. Many of my students see the doxa of race as objective, as do many groups and institutions. This is how the system of racialism is maintained and reproduced in Western society.

While there are no objective or scientific ways to study race, race impacts nearly every aspect of everyday life in the United States. Race is an inherently hierarchical system that unevenly allocates cultural, economic, political, social, and symbolic capital to groups and individuals. In order to understand the influence of race on the daily lives of people and its resulting effect on the archaeological record at Timbuctoo, it is necessary to understand the historical origins of racial thinking and the theoretical frameworks we use to understand race.

Race is both a social structure and an ideology. It is a social structure in that it was created and has been maintained through the collective actions of individuals. When the concept of race was created it was through the collective action of individuals who used physical and cultural characteristics to create categories of humans. Over time, as more individuals and groups came to internalize race as a perceived reality, it became a social structure that was used to socialize individuals into race as an ideology. I follow Althusser (1971, 127–186), who defines ideology as a construct that masks economic, political, and social inequalities. Ideologies about such inequalities are strategies that elites use to promote their own interests by sowing distrust and division among the masses (Leone 2005; Little and Shackel 2014). The ideology of race protects the interests of the elite by creating false boundaries between racialized groups so that they are set in opposition to each other and do not see their shared marginalization. Elites encourage racialized groups to see any economic, political, or social gains for one group as a direct threat to their interests. Despite the struggles marginalized groups share and the fact that their economic status and living conditions are often similar, the racialized ideology elites promote encourages groups to believe that only people with whom they share racial affiliation have the same types of experiences that they do (Leonardo 2005, 402).

This ideology of race was and still is used to quell any attempts at class solidarity in the United States (Smedley 1999, 119–122; Marx and Engels 2016; Roediger 2019, 97), leaving the power of the dominant classes unchallenged as the masses struggle against each other. Racial ideologies create new forms of repression between and among groups while also maintaining the preexisting social structure that distributes power unevenly. Marginalized groups view other racialized groups and individuals as the reason for their condition instead of taking action against the system that limits their economic, political, and social power.

The binary worldview of Enlightenment thinkers created codified binaries of white versus Black, superior versus inferior, and free versus enslaved (Pressly 2006, 84). As enslaved Africans and their descendants became the primary labor supply in the American Southeast, a connection between phenotypic traits and hierarchical labeling became the dominant discourse in America (Orser 2004, 2007). This ideology held that even if a Black person was "free," white people saw them as inferior no matter what their social or economic status was. This relationship between Black skin and slavery is illustrated in an incident involving Rev. Richard Allen, the founder of the African Methodist Episcopal Church (Barton 2012). Allen was born into slavery in Delaware, but over time he was able to purchase his freedom. He moved to Philadelphia and established a successful chimney-sweeping business, eventually becoming one of the most affluent Black men in the city. However, despite his affluence and influence, a slave catcher came to Allen's house in 1800 and accused him of being a runaway. Allen challenged the charge, but because a Black man could not give testimony in court, he was unable to speak for himself. It was not until Alderman

Alexander Todd, an affluent white Quaker, submitted testimony that he had known Allen for over twenty years that the court dismissed the slave catcher's accusation (Newman 2008).

Another case involved Solomon Northup, a free man from New York who was kidnapped and enslaved for over twelve years before he regained his freedom (Northup 1853). Both Allen and Northup were legally free, but because of the power of racial ideologies and the association whites made between Black phenotype and enslavement, they and others lived in a state of fear and uncertainty.

The oppositions of inferiority and superiority, of enslaved and free that were created through stereotypes about phenotypic traits helped reproduce the institution of racialized slavery. Although whites in the United States had already racialized Native Americans by the late 1600s, over the next centuries, they expanded the process of racialization to include people of Asian, Irish, and Jewish descent and other groups. However, for this book I focus on the Black-white dialectic that has dominated racial discourse and racism in the United States since the colonial era. White people's fears that the population of people of color, particularly Black people, would increase have resulted in systemic forms of racism designed to limit the ability of people of color to acquire various forms of capital. In 1691, white Virginians passed laws that made marriage between white people and Black people illegal and stated that the children of interracial intercourse were not white, which limited their social and political status. These laws drew upon the "one drop rule," whereby a person who had even one ancestor who was not white was legally considered to also be not white, regardless of the color of their skin (Orser 2007; Barton 2012). One of the reasons for these legal strategies was to protect white hegemony by perpetuating racialized slavery and by ensuring that interracial children would be unable to inherit the status and wealth of their white parents. These legal strategies expanded the economic, political, and social opportunities for those deemed "white" at the expense of Black people and had consequences for both free Black and enslaved people.

For free Black people, as we have seen in the Allen example, the effects of racism ensured that no matter how much economic or social capital they accumulated, white people would always connect their phenotype with racialized slavery and inferiority. Because slavery was racialized in the United States, white people could not be enslaved, thus cementing their ideology of white superiority leading up to the Civil War. Moreover, regardless of economic or social status, white people believed in their racial superiority (Roediger 1991, 13). Impoverished white people believed that they shared more with the middle- and upper-class whites than with people of color with whom they shared many economic, political, and social characteristics.

Paul Mullins (1999a) has demonstrated that after the end of slavery, racism against people of color, especially Black people, increased in the United States. In a capitalist society, economic capital is used as a measure of an individual's social and symbolic capital (Bourdieu 1986). It not entirely but mostly determines whether society sees a person as successful. This ideology became problematic in the context of late nineteenth-century America, where slavery no longer existed and Black people could compete with and even surpass white people in terms of the property they owned. Throughout the nineteenth century, the dominant belief among white elites was that if a white person was poor, it was not because of social conditions or the systemic injustices of capitalism, it was because of the individual's own moral failing. Prior to the end of slavery, if a Black person had this level of success, it did not matter for many whites as they could still rely on the ideological benefits that they were superior, but in the postbellum era these no longer existed. If a Black person could acquire economic capital—and thus social and symbolic capital—on their own, then the poverty a white person experienced was due to their own failure as an individual (Roediger 2019, 71).

The fears of white people that they would lose economic and political power worsened in 1870, when the Fifteenth Amendment stated that neither the federal nor state governments could deny a man the right to vote on the basis of his skin color. This gave Black men the potential power to bring about positive change for their community through their participation in suffrage. The fear was that there would no longer be any distinctions that separated the white middle and working classes from a Black population that five years earlier had been enslaved (Mullins 1999a, 22; Barton 2012).

White elites created legal and political institutional barriers to Black upward mobility throughout the United States in the second half of the nineteenth century. Examples include formal racial segregation in the South and informal segregation in the North. In northern cities, most white employers refused to hire Black workers and labor organizations excluded them. Racialized caricatures of Black people and other people of color became common in literature, advertising, and popular culture. Examples include postcards, blackface minstrel shows, and bric-a-brac (Barton and Somerville 2016). Racist organizations such as the Ku Klux Klan, the White League, and the Red Shirts terrorized Blacks in the South. Race-based riots and lynchings were also common. Scientific racism sought to prove the racial superiority of the white race (Gould 1996, 101–104; Barton 2012).

Sociologist W. E. B. Du Bois referred to white privilege as a form of compensation for white workers:

> While [whites] received a low wage, they were compensated in part by a sort of public and psychological wage. They were given public deference and titles of courtesy because they were white. They were admitted freely with all classes of white people to public functions, public parks, and the best schools. The police were drawn from their ranks, and the courts, dependent on their votes, treated them with such leniency as to encourage lawlessness. Their votes selected public officials, and while this had small effect upon their economic situation, it had great effect upon their personal treatment and the deference shown them. (Du Bois 1935, 700–701)

In a postslavery society, psychological wages created and reproduced the belief that the white race was socially and biologically superior to people of color. Like the ideology of individualism and the belief that social mobility was possible in a capitalist society, psychological wages were used to mask the systemic poverty many white people endured. Charles Orser (2004) writes that white elites created these belief systems to prevent any chance that class solidarity would develop between racial groups. Even poor white people benefited from the privileges of being white. They did not have to endure the negative aspects of segregation, most white men were not denied the ability to vote, and they could aspire toward upward economic and social mobility without fear of reprisals based on their race in the first half of the twentieth century. White people continue to benefit from a racialized society that rewards us with opportunities that often exclude people of color.

While white elites constructed the ideology of racial superiority, historically the white middle and working classes have been its strongest proponents (Diemer 2009). This is true today also. The white men who chanted "Jews will not replace us" in Charlottesville, Virginia, at the Unite the Right rally in August 2017 were not the economic or social elite; they were middle- and working-class men.[1] It is middle- and working-class white people, often not elite whites, who have repeatedly attempted to repeal affirmative action programs in colleges and universities; they believe that any gains people of color make are threats to their power.[2] Many white people see themselves as precariously caught between the dominant elite class and the poor masses. Many realize that they will never reach the upper echelons of society but fear that they are one unpaid medical bill or one missed mortgage payment away from slipping into poverty. It is important to note that from the time of the rise of consumerism in the early twentieth century, the middle class in the American psyche is not just an economic status; it is also a sociopolitical ideology (Fitts 1999; Mullins 2017, 92). In US society, where economic capital is inextricably tied with social capital, white fears of impoverishment also entail the threat of losing middle-class identity. Therefore, the perceived and real benefits of adhering to racial ideologies offer a sense of security through the demonization of impoverished people of color.

For example, a 2017 study by the Public Religion Research Institute found that it was fears of cultural displacement, not economic concerns, that drove white working-class Americans toward former president Donald Trump. According to the report, 65 percent of white working-class study participants believe that American culture has been deteriorating since the 1950s (Jones et al. 2017). Forty-eight percent said that "things have changed so much that I often feel like a stranger in my own country" (Jones et al. 2017). Fifty-two percent of white working-class participants believe that discrimination against whites is as big a problem as discrimination against people of color. These fears are the results of both sociopolitical progress made by people of color since the 1960s and the nefarious nature of late capitalism.

While the civil rights movement brought about advancement for African Americans, Native peoples, and women, it also led to a backlash. For example, in the early 1950s the Ku Klux Klan (KKK) had limited enrollment. But after 1954, when the US Supreme Court ruled against racial segregation in public schools, KKK membership increased. By 1965, it had an estimated 50,000 members throughout the South (Southern Poverty Law Center 2011, 25). While the KKK engaged in violent attacks on Black people in the South, conservative politicians elsewhere in the country employed racist threats against people of color (Brown 2004, 191).

By the 1970s, racist white people often saw women of color as lazy "welfare queens" who were taking advantage of the system at the expense of the white middle and working classes.[3] This was part of a continued trend of late capitalism in which white people argued that the willingness of people of color to work for lower wages than white men destabilized white men's wages (Roediger 1991). Employers frequently outsourced jobs in order to ensure that wages remained low and to bust unions in the early twentieth century (Shackel 2009).

In a capitalist society in which economic capital is conflated with social status, many members of the white middle and working classes internalize what they see as economic threats as attacks on white America. Some white middle- and working-class people use perceived threats from workers of color, particularly immigrants from Central America and Mexico, to propagate racism under the banner of "America First" (Yang 2018). The Public Religion Research Institute survey found that nearly 70 percent of white working-class people who supported Trump believed that their way of life in the United States needed to be protected from foreign influence (Jones et al. 2017). The same study found that 62 percent of white-working class respondents believed that immigrants threaten American culture. But as Mimi Yang notes of these perceived threats to "American culture," "Trump's 'America First' or Trumpism erects racial and cultural hierarchies and sets out to legitimize them, brings America to the pre–Civil Rights Movement era to 'make America great again,' sparks fear, bigotry, and distrust among Americans, and deepens the boundary between the two Americas. Trumpism is not Americanism, but a masqueraded white supremacism and nativism." These economic and sociopolitical fears stand in contrast to reality. For an example of an economic reality, in 2019, white workers earned 10.8 percent more than Hispanic workers and 14.9 percent more than Black workers (Gould 2020). And yet the public is still bombarded by racist rhetoric such as "They're taking our jobs. They're taking our manufacturing jobs. They're taking our money. They're killing us."[4]

An example of a reaction against the perceived attack on white sociopolitical hegemony can be seen in the 250 new laws that have been proposed in forty-three states designed to restrict voting rights. While the stated purpose of these laws is to "protect the integrity of elections," these restrictions will disproportionately affect voters of color.[5] These fears, threats, and reactions are very much rooted in racist ideologies.

This discussion of the history and legacies of race has focused only on the ideological frameworks of race. However, race is more than an ideology and racism is more than the actions of individuals and groups. Sociologist Eduardo Bonilla-Silva (1997) points out two problems when we study race and racism as ideologies. First, Bonilla-Silva agrees that race as an ideology originated during European colonialism as a by-product of class, but he argues that as race became more important in society, it developed into its own social structure. Studying race as an ideological construct means that we study it as a worldview that masks the reality that there are no biological categories of humans. This approach fails to address the truth that race permeates every aspect of our society. Race as a social structure is both institutional and part of everyday practice. For example, it is institutional in the ways that we interact with the government when we select our race during the census. In this way, the structure of race is reinforced and reproduced by our interactions with the government, higher education, healthcare—all the large institutions that make up our society. Additionally, race as a structure influences our everyday practices. These practices are the routine aspects of life that we often do not think about, the ways that we go through our daily lives (De Certeau 1984). Race affects our everyday lives not just through the ways that we interact with one another; it also influences the economic prospects, educational possibilities, and sociopolitical opportunities of individuals (Bonilla-Silva 1997).

Bonilla-Silva's second argument is that we too often focus on racism as a belief that individuals have moral failings rather than as a systemic structure (Bonilla-Silva 1997, 466; Orser 2004, 113–114). The media and most of the nation saw the white-supremacist Unite the Right rally in Charlottesville, Virginia, on August 11 and 12, 2017, as a display of racism. Burning crosses, waving Nazi flags, and chanting "The South Will Rise Again" are racist actions, but viewing these individual acts as the sum total of racism fails to take into account the structural racism in the United States that greatly affects the everyday lives of people of color. Mass incarceration of Black men, the stop-and-frisk policies of police around the country, unequal access of Black people to healthcare, and blocked access to economic opportunities are examples of the structural racism that Bonilla-Silva contends should be the focus of our studies. Studying ideological aspects of race and racism does not reveal the myriad ways that racism affects the everyday lives of people of color (Orser 2004, 114).

Mark Leone (2010, 23–24) points out that racist beliefs are "a way of establishing hierarchy so that unequally held wealth . . . is protected." Those who subscribe to racism believe that people of color have inherent qualities that justify hatred and that they deserve the poverty and exploitation they suffer because of those inherent qualities.

Structures and ideologies of race are not only reflections of a racialized society, they are also a constitutive element of society because they create an "organizational map that guides the actions of racial actors in society" (Bonilla-Silva 1997, 474). White people and people of color have a dialectical relationship because the existence of one group depends on its differences from the other (Orser 2004, 115). I like to host group exercises in my classes that illustrate this point. I ask students to give me examples of Black culture in America. Most of my students can rattle off numerous examples of Black culture such as food, music, language, and religion. Then I ask them to give me clear examples of white culture—not examples of ethnicity such as polka music or Irish dancing but universal practices of the white race. The students fall silent at this point. Next, I ask them about the section of the hair products aisle at the grocery store or drugstore labeled "ethnic" and ask them what label is used for the other products in that aisle. Most correctly say that there is no official label. I ask them if the section of "ethnic" hair care products is predominantly for people with "black hair," then who is the other unnamed section for? Most of my students reply that it is for "white people." This exercise helps students understand how white and whiteness are defined as normal or the natural state in US society. The white race is not defined by its own characterizations or traits; it is defined by what it is not. The white race in the United States has been created and maintained through a backdoor process of defining the "other" (Barton and Somerville 2016). Examples include equating phenotype with enslavement, laws that defined race using one-drop rules, and the absence of universal characteristics of "white culture." Whiteness is seen as normal, as the status quo in our society. This is the power of the white race, that it is everywhere, yet you can never truly point your finger on what defines it. The fact that whiteness is ambiguous by design does not decrease its power and the ways that it affects everyday practices.

The archaeology of Timbuctoo requires an understanding of the intersectionality of race and class. Although our understanding of race in the United States was developed within the context of economic class and slavery, as race became internalized in society it developed into its own social structure (Bonilla-Silva 1997; Roediger 2019). As a pervasive structure, race affected the everyday lives of the individuals who lived in Timbuctoo. Race influenced their ability to acquire cultural, economic, political, and symbolic capital. White people limited the opportunities of Black residents for betterment, such as jobs that paid higher wages. This brings us back to the separate yet intertwined structures of race and class (Cerroni-Long 1987). Each system influences the other and both systems affect the experiences and practices of individuals and thus shaped the archaeological record. The archaeology of Timbuctoo is a study of poverty that is not attributable to the moral failings of individuals or an unwillingness to work. It is attributable to the social structures of a racialized society.

HISTORY OF TIMBUCTOO

There is a lot in a name. Names have meaning for the name givers and sometimes those meanings can be passed on to others. Names highlight a place over space; they are used to highlight the uniqueness of one location against others (Rothman and Savulis 2003). For people of the African Diaspora, the name Timbuktu represents the global marketplace in Mali that flourished in the fourteenth through sixteenth centuries, an example of what Africans outside the system of European imperialism could do. For Black people in the United States, Timbuktu, Mali, has been a symbol of the power and perseverance.[1] Timbuktu, spelled in various ways, is the name of three other American settlements outside New Jersey: Timbuctoo, California (founded in the 1850s), Timbuktu, Oregon (founded in the late 1800s), and Timbuctoo, New York (established in 1846). The name was used in the nineteenth century because of a white orientalist ideology that saw Timbuktu as a place of "otherness," mystery, and veneration (Dubois 1896).

People still use the name Timbuktu to signify a distant, remote, and exotic location. When I was a kid, my mom told me many times that she was going to send me to Timbuktu if I didn't stop being a pain. The name Timbuktu was also used in a variety of media, including literature, advertising, and children's toys, to emphasize an identity other than whiteness (Barton and Somerville 2012). In New Jersey, the whites likely used the name Timbuctoo in a manner to create an identity that segregated the members of the Black community from their white neighbors.

Despite years of research, we still do not know who named the community or why. One possible interpretation is that the community wanted a great name to inspire residents. That is what happened at the Timbuctoo in

New York, where it appears that the name of an interracial community that was associated with the abolitionist John Brown was rooted in admiration for the African city (Adirondack History Center 2002, 4). At the community in New Jersey, it is possible that the Black residents knew of the great Timbuktu and wanted to name their settlement after it.

A second possible origin of the name is a bit more negative and may be the result of white racist ideology. White people associated the name Timbuktu with an isolated, mysterious place, a place that was called a civilization but was not "civilized." In this view, the name Timbuctoo may have been used to signify a place as the "other." The normalization of whiteness in US society means that most white people label any deviation from that norm as different. We know that white residents of Northampton, New Jersey (now known as Mount Holly) saw Timbuctoo as different from the white-controlled spaces and places that surrounded it. We see this in newspaper accounts of Timbuctoo that used negative language to code its residents racially. In 1858, when a group of slave catchers kidnapped a Black resident, the headline in the *New Jersey Mirror* read "Trouble among the Darkies."[2] The two important words here are "darkies," a racist labeling of the Black residents, and "among," which both implies a collective identity and suggests a degree of separation between Timbuctoo and surrounding white communities. Another example is the racist naming of a historically Black neighborhood on Washington Street in Mount Holly as "N—— Hill," again underscoring an identity of "other" through a horrible racist slur, while also suggesting a separation of the Black place from the white surrounding space.

We do not have evidence to support either of these theories about how Timbuctoo, New Jersey, got its name. There can be several reasons why the community got its name that are not mutually exclusive and that meant different things for different people in different times.

History of Timbuctoo

Even when people are enslaved, they have power to resist their oppressors and in some way take back some control over their lives. Because of this reality, I do not use the word "slave" to describe a person in bondage. Instead, I use "enslaved" or "captive." While enslavers in the United States sought to control the bodies and minds of the people they held captive, they did not have the power to enslave their spirits or to determine their own desires.

Enslaved people had the agency and ability to resist. Not all forms of resistance were violent. Work slowdowns, equipment sabotage, and private religious practices are examples of resistance; of the agency of captives to push back against their oppressors (Weik 2012). To say that an individual had only one identity as a "slave," that they did not have any ability to have some control over their life, misrepresents the past and does that person an injustice. This is not a semantic issue. The decision to use "enslaved" or "captive person" over slave relates to an idea that is at the very heart of this work, that people have the ability to persevere and triumph over evil.

In 1826, formerly enslaved and likely "runaways" David, Ezekiel, and Wardell Parker and Hezekiah Hall from Maryland established the community of Timbuctoo in New Jersey (see figure 3.1). In September 1826, Ezekiel Parker purchased 1.4 acres from Quaker William Hilyard, a white businessman, for $22.16. Wardell Parker paid Hilyard $24.05 for 1.5 acres that same month. Hezekiah Hall purchased half an acre for $8.33 and David Parker bought 1 acre from Hilyard for $15.40. However, the name Timbuctoo did not appear on a deed until 1830 (Weston 2018, 2–3).

Timbuctoo's population grew because of natural reproduction, a state law of 1804 that gradually manumitted enslaved people, and the fact that the community was a station on the Underground Railroad. As people moved into the area, they had families and the population grew. But how and why did people move to Timbuctoo?

One reason was the gradual emancipation laws of New Jersey. New Jersey had a complex history with regard to slavery and Black people. In 1804, it was the last of the northern states to pass gradual manumission legislation. "An Act for the Gradual Abolition of Slavery" stated that all enslaved females born after July 4, 1804, were to be apprentices to their mother's captor until the age of 21 and that all males who were enslaved would be freed at the age of 25.[3] This meant that the first generation of manumitted people in New Jersey aged out of bondage around the time when Timbuctoo was founded. The state's gradual manumission law likely led to population growth in Timbuctoo and in other communities in the state.

In 1830, more than one-third of the 3,568 enslaved people living in the northern states were held in New Jersey (Marrin 2007, 328). Even by 1860, despite the Gradual Abolition Act of 1804, New Jersey still had eighteen enslaved people, who were listed as "Apprenticed for Life" (Wright 1989, 27). Much of the resistance to abolition in New Jersey came from the northern portion of the state, where textile manufacturers depended on enslaved

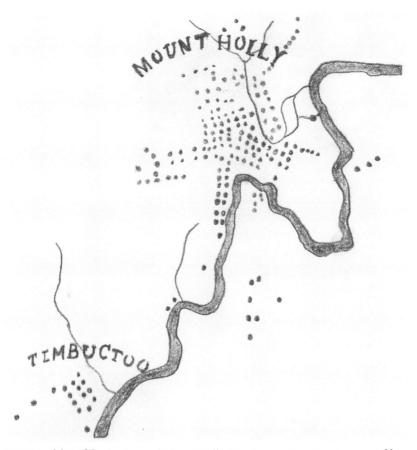

Figure 3.1. Map of Timbuctoo and Mount Holly, New Jersey, 1849. Drawing created by Christopher P. Barton. Source: Burlington County Historical Society.

labor in the South for cotton, and clothing manufacturers relied on southern planters to buy their goods. The state was so pro-slavery that it did not ratify the Thirteenth Amendment abolishing racialized slavery; instead it pushed for states' rights. But pro-slavery was not as common in the southern parts of the state, where Quakers were the dominant economic, political, and social force.

A third reason the population of Timbuctoo grew was the community's role as a terminus on the Underground Railroad. The Underground Railroad was not a "thing"; it was both an individual's belief that they could become free and the collective practices of groups and individuals who offered the means to get that freedom. The origin of the name Underground Railroad is not known. One folktale is that it was first used by a slave catcher who lost his target during a chase and claimed that the person had vanished into some underground railroad (Mingus 2016). It is more likely that it was used to symbolize two core aspects of the networks to freedom. First, "underground" implies a collectively held secret that is unknown to the masses. Participating in the Underground Railroad was extremely dangerous for the enslaved people seeking freedom and illegal for the free persons who worked to assist them. For example, the Fugitive Slave Act of 1850 mandated six months in prison and a $1,000 fine for anyone who helped a person who was escaping their captor. This is likely why there is scant documentation and almost no archaeological evidence for the Underground Railroad at Timbuctoo or elsewhere (see Delle 2008; Weik 2012; LaRoche 2014). But there are hints of Timbuctoo's role as a station on the Underground Railroad in newspaper accounts and census records, as I explain below.

The term Underground Railroad emphasizes two key ideas. First, the railroad—that is, the transportation system—was a vast system of land travel in the nineteenth century, suggesting that the escape to freedom would draw from a complex network of people and places. However, many of the Underground Railroad routes, especially in New Jersey, ran along the waterways (Wright 1989, 39–41). Wilbur H. Siebert (1898, 81–82) wrote that "the advantages of escape by boat were early discerned by slaves living near the coast or along inland rivers. Vessels engaged in our coastwise trade became more or less involved in transporting fugitives from Southern ports to Northern soil." Famous escapes by Frederick Douglass (1849) and Robert Smalls (Miller 1995) made by using waterways highlight the benefits of water travel.

The location of Timbuctoo on the Rancocas Creek was no accident. The creek, which is wide enough to accommodate canoes and small boats, is a tributary of the Delaware River, which flows into the Delaware Bay, a natural boundary between New Jersey and the slaveholding states of the Eastern shores of Delaware, Maryland, and Virginia. For escaping people, the Delaware Bay was a pathway to freedom. Timbuctoo is also close to the Quaker stronghold of Mount Holly. This settlement pattern was found throughout antebellum southern New Jersey: Black communities were founded near towns with sizable Quaker populations. Quakers dominated the economy, politics, and society of southern New Jersey. At nearly every historic Quaker town in southern New Jersey, you will find both a Black community and a waterway nearby (see figure 3.2). This network of the Underground Railroad, known as the Greenwich Line, extended from Greenwich, New Jersey, near the Delaware Bay through the Quaker-controlled areas of western New Jersey all the way up to New York City (Wright 1989, 39–40; see figure 3.2).

However, the Societies of Friends were not always proponents of abolition. From the early seventeenth century into the eighteenth century, Quakers were slaveowners; the Society of Friends recommended only that captors provide religious guidance to the people they enslaved (Cadbury 1936; Gigantino 2014). However, Quaker attitudes about slavery shifted in the latter half of the eighteenth century, when some members began to argue that the practice went against their Christian beliefs (Fishman 1997, 195–196). This change of heart was rooted in the actions of several Quaker leaders, most notably in New Jersey in the work of John Woolman.

A resident of Mount Holly in Burlington County, New Jersey, Woolman became the foremost vocal Quaker abolitionist in the region. When Woolman was a young clerk, a Quaker client asked him to draft a bill of sale for an enslaved man in 1742. Woolman wrote that the event changed his life, stating in his journal that "writing an instrument of slavery for one of my fellow creatures felt uneasy." This led him to resolve that "slave-keeping [was] a practice inconsistent with the Christian religion" (quoted in Slaughter 2008, 103; see also Gigantino 2014, 21–22) This event started Woolman on a path that eventually led him to become the leader of the abolitionist movement among the Quakers (Gigantino 2014, 21–23). Although the Society of Friends had mostly denounced the practice of slavery in the late eighteenth century, at the 1774 Yearly Meeting in Philadelphia, the society started to ban the practice of slavery by its members. After the 1776 meeting, the society decreed that it would end the membership of any Quaker who continued to enslave people (Gigantino 2014, 21–22). This was a major step in American abolitionism. However, this fact also helped link the Quaker religion to the authorized public history of the antislavery movement and the Underground Railroad. Classroom textbooks and historical markers often identify Quakers as the primary "operators" of the Underground Railroad.

These accounts simplify Quakers' varying attitudes toward slavery and overemphasize their roles while excluding evidence of Black agency in the story of the Underground Railroad. Donna McDaniel and Vanessa Julye (2008, 97) note that active participation in the abolitionist movement

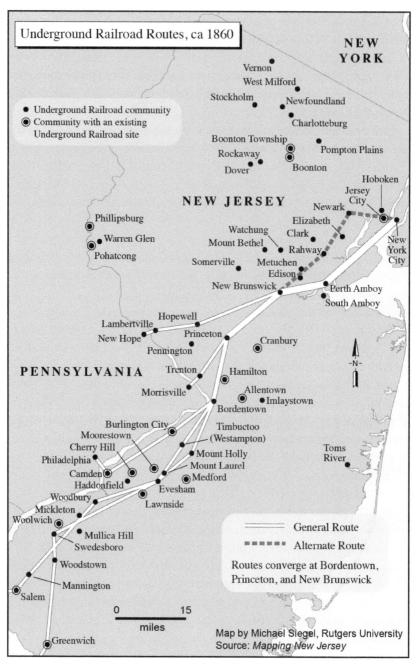

Figure 3.2. Map of the Greenwich Line of the Underground Railroad. Created by Michael Siegel, adapted from the original color map in "*Steal Away, Steal Away*": *A Guide to the Underground Railroad in New Jersey* (Trenton: New Jersey Historical Commission, 2002). Source: Michael Siegel.

among Quakers was limited and that other Christian denominations were as active as Quakers. In the mid-nineteenth century, while most Quakers were against slavery for religious reasons, they were ambivalent about active participation in the Underground Railroad. Larry Gara (1961, 18) argues that the accounts and widely held beliefs that Quakers were "operators" of the Underground Railroad were the result of the participation of "a small number of Friends." McDaniel and Julye (2008, 97–98, 28) attribute the exaggerated role that Quakers enjoy regarding the Underground Railroad to three reasons. First, the early stand of the Society of Friends against slavery created the perception that not only were they against enslavement but that all Quakers were active in the Underground Railroad. Second, many escapees traveled through routes that took them through Philadelphia and its surrounding areas, including southern New Jersey, a region that was heavily populated by Quakers. Finally, the popularity of Harriet Beecher Stowe's *Uncle Tom's Cabin* created a public perception of activism on the part of the Society of Friends.

It is true that some Quakers were involved in the activities of the Underground Railroad. A number of Quakers did assist by passing along information and sheltering and the transportation of escaping people. The Society of Friends also helped educate white people about the horrors of slavery and raised funds to support the abolition movement. But it was Black people and Black churches that performed the daily activities that were necessary to help people escape from slavery. Cheryl LaRoche (2014) contends that the Underground Railroad was not a uniform network of routes but a frame of mind from which Black churches operated as the physical and spiritual center for the movement. However, Quakers offered financial and legal support for Black abolitionists and runaway people (Delle 2008; Barton and Markert 2012, 88).

The relationships between the white and Black communities in and near Mount Holly were complex. Quakers were adamant opponents of slavery and used their political capital to petition against the institution, their legal capital to represent self-freed people, and their economic capital to support abolitionist organizations (McDaniel and Julye 2008). However, most Quakers did not participate in the Underground Railroad and most did not consider Black people their social equals (Gigantino 2014, 70).

McDaniel and Julye (2008, 110) argue that the antislavery beliefs of many Quakers were not rooted in empathy for captives but in a sense of guilt for their previous participation in and profiting from slavery (see also

Gigantino 2014, 71; Hodges 1997, 74–75). Some Quakers feared that if they allowed slavery to continue they would be damned in the afterlife (Gigantino 2014, 71; McDaniel and Julye 2008, 31). Gary Nash and Jean Soderlund (1991, 54) argue that "Friends who had little humanitarian concern for blacks took up antislavery ideology in the hope that purging the Society of sin would pacify an angry God." Even after formerly enslaved Black people settled in or near Quaker communities, their Quaker neighbors did not view them as social and racial equals. While in the eighteenth and early nineteenth centuries some Black people were allowed to attend segregated services in Quaker Meeting Houses, they were continuously denied equal membership (Cadbury 1936, 168).

An example can be drawn from the life of William Boen (1735–1824). In 1763, when Boen was 28, he successfully negotiated his freedom and continued to live in the Mount Holly area as a practicing (but not an official) member of the Society of Friends (Gummere 1922; Cadbury 1936). Boen was publicly seen as a righteous man, and on his wedding day he petitioned the society for full membership. However, despite the recommendation of John Woolman, the society denied Boen full membership because of his race (Gummere 1922, 89; Cadbury 1936). Throughout his life he continued to request admission, but Boen was not admitted into the Mount Holly Society of Friends until 1814, when he was 79.

Mount Holly Friends selected a Black man (likely Boen), whom Woolman had endorsed, as a new elder in their society. However, the committee replied that they would have preferred to have no elder than to have a Black man as elder (Cadbury 1936). It was common for the Society of Friends to deny Black people membership, which suggests that most antislavery Quakers were more interested in saving themselves from damnation than they were in freeing their fellow brothers and sisters (Hodges 1997, 75).

But even if Quakers were motivated to participate in antislavery activities by a desire to save their own souls, Black people in the area welcomed their assistance. Quakers were on the forefront of pushing for manumission, for education for enslaved people, and for instituting fines for captors who abused captives. Even though most Quakers did not view Black people as their equals, the many types of economic, legal, and political assistance they provided helped both enslaved and free Black people.

Land was one of the greatest resources local Quakers offered residents of Timbuctoo. In addition to the land William Hilyard sold the first residents of Timbuctoo, Samuel Atkinson, Abigail Haywood, Thomas Grissom Sr., and Thomas Grissom Jr. sold lots that enabled the community to expand in the 1820s and 1830s. Peter Quire and John Bruer (also spelled Brewer) subdivided their lots to help establish the African Union School in 1834 and the School & Place of Divine Worship in 1841 for the residents of Timbuctoo. Although the plots of land Quakers sold Black residents were too small for intensive agriculture, they gave people a place where they could build their homes.

Quakers also provided jobs for the people of Timbuctoo. However, most of the work they offered was low-paying manual labor and/or domestic service. Male residents of the town found employment in local brickyards and as farmhands. According to census records, many of the women worked as domestic servants for white women and as laundresses from their own homes. A racialized landscape meant that Black people were consigned to the lower ends of the economic, political, and social spectrums.

Despite the complex relationship Quakers had with their Black neighbors, many remained the most ardent white supporters of the Underground Railroad and of Black people. While much of the white population in the state continued to work to prevent Black residents of the state from making social and/or political gains, Quakers influenced antislavery legislation (Gigantino 2014, 72). In 1786, legislation supported by Quakers overturned a law that required slaveholders to pay a £200 fee if they manumitted an enslaved person if they were over 35 years old and were able to provide for themselves. The 1786 legislation also mandated that all slaveowners teach enslaved people how to read and write and fined owners who failed to do so. The progressive steps forward encountered pushback, though. The same 1786 law stated that free Black people from other states could not enter New Jersey and required all free Black residents who traveled outside their hometown to carry a document that proved that they were free. In southern New Jersey, the population of free Black people grew from 5,524 individuals in 1840 to 9,853 people in 1860. Because white policymakers feared that these changing demographics meant that they would lose political influence, in 1807, they made an amendment to the New Jersey constitution that limited voting rights to white males (Klinghoffer and Elkis 1992, 164).

This range of practices in the state enables us to better understand the social networks that existed around Timbuctoo before the Civil War. The isolated, rural environment of Timbuctoo provided some protection, but residents still had to keep an eye out for slave catchers and their spies. In

1858, shots were fired by Timbuctoo residents into the home of William Spry, a Black man who some suspected of spying for slave catchers in Maryland.[4] The shots were attributed to three Timbuctoo residents: David "King" Parker (the leader of Timbuctoo), Perry Simmons, and William Chase. This event showcases the extremes that the residents were willing to go to in order to protect their community against perceived threats, including from people of color.

In 1860, former Timbuctoo Black resident Caleb Wright aided slave catcher George Alberti and his patrol in their attempt to arrest Perry Simmons, a self-freed man from Maryland who had been living in the area near the community. Simmons armed himself and hid with his family in their loft. Gunfire between Simmons and his pursuers ensued and amid all the commotion and shouting, Alberti and his posse saw a group of well-armed Black people coming to help Simmons. This incident, known as the Battle of Pine Swamp, was not the only example of slave catchers and their spies preying on Timbuctoo residents.[5] Because of the persistent threat of capture, the people of Timbuctoo were highly suspicious of outsiders, both white and Black. It was not uncommon for impoverished Black people to be paid by slave catchers as spies to inform against people who had freed themselves (Jackson 2019, 60).

Such acts of violence were not the only means of defense residents of Timbuctoo had. Census records provide evidence of a covert tactic residents used to protect themselves from slave catchers. The 1850 census was the first to ask for a person's place of origin. In 1850 and 1860, while fugitive slave laws were in effect, several Timbuctoo residents told the census taker that they had been born in New Jersey or some other northern state. However, in 1870, five years after slavery ended, those same people reported that they had in fact been born in slaveholding southern states. For example, James Hill was 40 years old when the census taker came to his door in 1850. If he had been born in New Jersey, he would have been legally free because of the 1804 Gradual Emancipation Act. He told the census taker that he was born in New Jersey. But in 1870 there was no longer a need to give a false origin, so when the census taker asked for his place of birth, Hill answered that he had been born in Virginia. Table 3.1 shows the names, ages, and state of origin for people who changed their answer about place of birth from 1850 to 1870.

This pattern suggests that residents of Timbuctoo were communicating with one another about how to talk to the census taker as a form of protec-

Table 3.1. Census interpretations from Timbuctoo

Name	1850 State of Origin	Age	1860 State of Origin	Age	1870 State of Origin	Age	Change in State of Origin	Possible Fugitive
James A. Hill	NJ	40	PA	50	VA	58	X	X
David Roan	NJ	34			MD	53	X	X
Richard Christy	NJ	28	MD	45	MD	55	X	X
Sarah			MD	40	DE	48	X	X
Stephen Simmons	NJ	30			MD	52	X	X
Raimon (Raymond) Jones	NJ	30	DE	40	MD	46	X	X
Catharine	NJ	24	DE	38	DE	41	X	X
Atta (Adda) (Attie) Armstrong	NJ	38	NJ	65	MD	67	X	X
Elizabeth Mitchel	NJ	44	NJ	45	MD	55	X	X
Elizabeth Parker	NJ	51	DE	75	MD	82	X	X
Morris Gaines	NJ	5			DE	25	X	X
Elizabeth Hamilton			MA	30	MD	44	X	X
John Brown	DE	41			MD	54	X	?
William Nolon (Noland?)	NJ	32	DE	40	MD	60	X	X
John Sa(u?)nders	NJ	50	PA	65	MD	70	X	X
Anna	NJ	56	PA	55	MD	65	X	X
David Parker	NJ	50			MD	69	X	X

Sources: 1850 Federal Census for Westampton, Burlington County, New Jersey, Ancestry.com, citing National Archives and Records Administration microfilm roll 443, pages 275–276; 1860 Federal Census for Westampton, Burlington County, New Jersey, Ancestry.com, citing National Archives and Records Administration, pages 614–616; 1870 Federal Census for Westampton, Burlington County, New Jersey, Ancestry.com, citing National Archives and Records Administration, page 662B.

tion. It is interesting to note that of the seventeen possible self-freed people, thirteen were from Maryland, the same state the founders of Timbuctoo had fled. This reading of the census suggests that people who escaped captivity knew that Timbuctoo was a place where they might be safe. However, that safety was not guaranteed. Historian Paul Schopp (2012; personal communication, February 14, 2012) argues that because of frequent visits from slave catchers, the community's population ebbed and flowed as residents left their homes to find safer areas. These covert and overt practices show the lengths Timbuctoo residents would go to in order to secure their freedom.

The willingness of the people of Timbuctoo to protect others is seen in men's enlistment into the United States Colored Troops (USCT). The men of Timbuctoo served in the 6th, 22nd, 25th, and 29th Infantry Regiments of the USCT. Most experienced combat (Astle 2008). Today, the gravestones of the USCT soldiers are some of the only aboveground markers that remain of the nineteenth-century residents of the community. The home of William Davis, a USCT veteran, and his family became the focal point of our community-based archaeological work.

The community reached its peak in the years leading up to and immediately after the Civil War, as the protection and potential for employment the community provided offered a welcome respite for formerly enslaved people. At the start of the Civil War, in 1860, the population of Timbuctoo reached around 125 (Lyght 1978, 38–39). The community supported houses, outbuildings, a schoolhouse, an African Methodist Episcopal Zion Church, and a nearby general store (Turton 1999; Barton and Markert 2012, 82).

The Black community of Marshalltown in Salem County, New Jersey, had a similar history. Founded in 1834 by Thomas Marshall (1803–1856), the community was located in the Haines Neck portion of Mannington Township (Sheridan 2013, 31). The community has also been called "Marlboro," for the nearby marl mines where some residents worked, and "Frogtown," a reference to the tidal marshes near the community. Marshalltown supported a church, two cemeteries (African Union and African Methodist Episcopal), a store, a school, and several homesteads. Like Timbuctoo, Marshalltown grew as the result of manumissions after the 1804 act and as Black people purchased land there around 1834 (Sheridan 2013, 32–35). While some freedpeople migrated to more progressive northern states (and Canada) after manumission, others moved into Black enclaves such as Timbuctoo and Marshalltown that offered protection, support, and a sense of collective identity.

Although there is no direct written evidence to link Marshalltown to the Underground Railroad, we know that the freedom network was very active in Salem County (Sheridan 2013, 38–41). Salem County's location along the Delaware River and Delaware Bay offered people escaping the slave states of Delaware and Maryland routes to freedom. Sheridan notes that the isolation of Marshalltown, where there were no railroads, canals, stagecoaches, or deep-water rivers for steamboat travel, made the community a good location for people who did not want to be found. The only entrances to the community were a poorly constructed dirt road and the tidal upstream currents that led to the shallow creeks at Hook Bridge or Kates Creek Meadow (40–41). In 1850, the 756 Black residents of Mannington, of which Marshalltown was a part, accounted for 35 percent of the total population of the town. Nineteen percent of Black residents reported that they had been born in Maryland, Delaware, Virginia, and South Carolina. Sheridan (40) posits that this is evidence that runaway captives came to the area by the Underground Railroad and decided to stay.

Another similarity in the histories of Timbuctoo and Marshalltown is the presence and support of local Quakers. Salem County has long been associated with Quakers; the first meeting house in Salem was established in 1675. Quakers in the Marshalltown area offered support and employment at nearby homesteads, in the marl mine, and on farms (Sheridan 2013, 45). Although these jobs offered low pay, they gave the Black residents of Marshalltown income they could use to build their lives. However, for much of the community's existence until the 1950s, Marshalltown residents remained on the lower end of the economic and social spectrums.

At Timbuctoo also, poverty continued to be an issue (Barton and Markert 2012, 89–90). In 1890, the annual report of the New Jersey State Board of Education (1890, 14) stated that the "colored" school at Timbuctoo was closed during most of the 1889 school year due to a lack of funding. The board reported in 1896 that attendance was poor at the Timbuctoo "colored" school because "late in the fall and early spring the children are sent out to earn if possible their daily bread" (New Jersey State Board of Education 1897, 111). The 1896 report also recommended that the schoolhouse be closed because of its dilapidated condition.

These reports reveal several things about the poverty of the Timbuctoo community. First, the economic situation of families meant that children had to work, which limited their opportunities for formal education. Second, the schoolhouse's dilapidated condition and lack of funding highlight the community's economic struggles.

One former resident of Timbuctoo recalled his father's lack of education and the type of work he did as a school-age child in the 1930s:

> Then I came back here and my father raised a lot of pigs, man. We came from school, had to go out there and feed them pigs. That whole field out there was full of pigs, man. Had pigs out there, had pigs down there. I used to dread it because I knew I had to come home and feed them pigs and we had to clean them pigpens out, god dog!
>
> Like I said, my father couldn't read and write. My mother taught him how to write his name. My father made himself a pushcart and he'd take this pushcart and go into town, and we'd go in there and get garbage, and trash with that pushcart and we'd bring it down to feeds these hogs, man. After school I would help him push that pushcart. (Quoted in Barton et al. 2013, 202)

In this quote, we can see how a family needed the labor of children to survive.

Education became a source of success and pride. Several of the elders who gave oral histories were the first in their family to graduate from high school. But racism was an ever-present issue at school.

> I ain't gonna call the names of the KKK but I knew who they were. I mean, we learned who they were. They're from Rancocas, and Rancocas was known for its prejudice, man, and they would call you n——— in a minute. Well, they heard it from their parents, you know what I mean. We went to school together, we'd all catch the bus together, but we didn't get along, and I'll never forget [name omitted], she had a black spaniel, border spaniel, and they called him n———.
>
> And man, one day we were going to Rancocas, on the bus, and she seen her dog, she didn't know no better, she said Here, "n———, n———, n———," and we's like? [Laughter breaks out among the elders]
>
> Cause that was the name of the dog, that the family gave her, you know what I mean. It was a surprise to hear that. She was innocent, you know what I mean, she didn't know better. (Quoted in Barton et al. 2013, 207–208)

The white child was socialized to make the connection between the dog's black color and a slur that was meant for Black people. Even though the elder stated that the white child was unaware of what the slur meant and did not mean to offend, the Black children on the school bus were well socialized to understand the networks of race and racism. This memory shows both the omnipresence of racism in the area and how Black children were socialized by their families to understand the threats and dangers of the world. Through hearing the stories about slavery, the children came to understand that racism was everywhere, even in the names of pets.

Racism and barriers to economic and social upward mobility kept the residents of Timbuctoo in poverty throughout the twentieth century (Interracial Committee, New Jersey Department of Institutions and Agencies 1932, 12). This is the period of most of the archaeological evidence at Timbuctoo. What became clear through written records, oral histories, and archaeology is the unique collective identities and practices people developed at Timbuctoo. These collective identities center on the intersectionality of race and class, which is highlighted in the social memories and individual experiences of the former residents.

Paul Shackel (2003, 3) discusses how social memories, including oral histories, are created to promote collective identity and unity. He notes that individuals use social memories to create an exclusionary past in which a group remembers or deliberately forgets select elements of the past in order to construct unity.

There is a strong sense of community identity among the elders at Timbuctoo, although the definition of who is and who is not from "Bucktoe," as many call it, varies with each individual. Some descendants do not consider people who have ancestors who lived there but have never lived there themselves to be part of the community. However, all of the elders share the story of the Hanging Tree. Now no one knows which tree it is, but residents and former residents know the story. As children, they were told that when the slave trade was active in the Timbuctoo area, slave catchers would hang captives from a particular tree. They also heard of nearby caves along the creek that still have slave shackles hanging from the walls or of shallow graves of runaway captives in the woods. These claims have often been dismissed as anecdotal and there is no documented evidence of the slave trade running through Timbuctoo and no accounts of slave catchers executing people in the community. In fact, it was not typical for slave catchers to kill "runaways" because their goal was to return people to bondage. Nor is it at all likely that a tree still stands in the community that is old enough to date to the nineteenth century and we know that the caves with shackles do not exist because there are no caves along the Rancocas Creek.

However, these stories served an important purpose. Many of the elders who retell these memories learned them in the early to mid-twentieth century during a period when the Ku Klux Klan (KKK) was active in the county and New Jersey was racially segregated. Adults told these stories to children to teach them about the brutal experiences of slavery and the realities of their current situation, which included institutional racism in the forms of racial segregation and the presence of the KKK in the area.

Some elders told the story of a schoolyard fight between a white child from outside the community and a black child from Timbuctoo. The fight was a simple schoolyard tussle that ended with neither of the children injured. However, members of the KKK came to Timbuctoo seeking retribution because a Black child had dared to fight with a white child (Barton and Markert 2012, 91; Barton et al. 2013, 27). Informed of a potential "race riot," the police quickly came to the community and were able to stop the two sides before any violence broke out. Another resident told us that when she was a child, she was awakened in the middle of the night by the sight of a cross burning in the family's yard (Barton and Markert 2012, 89; Barton et al. 2013, 27–28).

The presence of the KKK in and around the area runs counter to the widely held public beliefs that New Jersey was a liberal, progressive state regarding race relations (Barton and Markert 2012, 89–90). While New Jersey and particularly Burlington County had white residents who were in the forefront of abolitionism in the eighteenth and nineteenth centuries, the KKK was popular in the state by the twentieth century. For example, in the 1920s, the median time period for our artifact assemblage, the New Jersey chapters of the KKK had an estimated 60,000 to 100,000 members (Linderoth 2010, 69). At a rally in Brook Bound in 1923, some 40 miles north of Timbuctoo, over 12,000 uniformed KKK members paraded through the city's streets.[6] In the same year at Allenwood, 40 miles east of Timbuctoo, over 1,500 people attended a rally called the "Women of the Klan."[7] In 1926, Margaret Sanger, a noted American eugenicist, was a guest speaker for the women's branch of the KKK rally in Silver Lake just 30 miles south of Timbuctoo (Sanger 2010, 366). These events place Timbuctoo in the epicenter of activities for the KKK in New Jersey in the first half of the twentieth century. These rallies convey the KKK's popularity. They underscore how openly the white public supported it, but it was the anonymity created by the hoods the members wore that created fear among Black people. The hoods were a strategy the KKK used to terrorize their targets; any white person a Black person knew could be a member of the KKK. When placed in this historical context, we can see why stories such as the one about the Hanging Tree were told and retold to underscore the experiences of slavery and racism in order to form a collective identity that taught Black people to be aware of their surroundings at all times.

This identity was created through the experiences of the group. While each individual had a worldview that was uniquely shaped by their own experiences, the group shared a common core of experiences. At Timbuctoo, the structures of race and class created and maintained a habitus of making do. But while it is important to discuss the omnipresence of race and class for residents and former residents, in interviews, residents and former residents emphasized that hardships did not harden their memories of the past (Barton and Markert 2012). For many people, Timbuctoo is a place of pride. As one resident said, "That was a place you could be proud of, your home. It was your roots" (quoted in Barton et al. 2013). All of the former residents we interviewed spoke of the daily struggles of poverty, of working hard and "having nothing," but each person emphasized that "Bucktoe" was a close-knit community: "It was a nice village then, we all got along. All of them had families. . . . So we all took care of each other, all looked out for each other, and if you all got in trouble, the other one would know about it" (quoted in Barton et al. 2013). The collective identity of belonging to the physical space of Timbuctoo intersected with the reality of being impoverished and Black. This created a collective ethos in which community members assisted one another with everything from daily work and sharing meals after church service to delivering babies. Through this collective ethos, the impoverished community was able to create a system of mutual assistance. Marginalized communities commonly build such support systems to help each other cope with the adverse effects of poverty and oppression (Goode and Maskovsky 2002; Scheper-Hughes 1992). Even today, the aging former residents and residents of Timbuctoo continue to stand as testaments to this collective action of resistance, perseverance, and triumphs. Even though today much of the 60 acres that once included Timbuctoo have been covered by suburban sprawl and many of the residents have moved on, a dedicated group of stakeholders remains who are invested in the history and future of Timbuctoo.

The Davis Site

William Davis was born free in the township of Northampton in 1836 (Westampton was created when Northampton was divided in 1850). In adulthood he worked as a brick molder at one of the nearby brickyards. In 1863, when he was 27, Davis enlisted in the 22nd USCT Infantry Regiment

(Astle 2008). He was gravely wounded in the chest at the Battle of Petersburg, Virginia, and was honorably discharged in 1864. Davis suffered rheumatism and back pain from his war wound for the rest of his life, which limited the work he could do. The Dependent and Disability Pension Act of 1890 created pensions for wounded veterans like Davis who were unable to perform manual labor because of physical disabilities (Astle 2008). However, Davis continued to work. In 1910, he told the census taker that he was employed as a manual laborer despite his condition and age.

According to historical documents, the Davis property was once owned by David "King" Parker, the leader of Timbuctoo. Mary Simmons, a relative of Perry Simmons, acquired the property after Parker died. On September 20, 1879, the executors of Simmons's estate sold the lot to William Davis and his wife, Rebecca, for two dollars (Turton 1999). The one-story home constructed on the property was built on top of a 12 × 16-foot brick foundation. There are no photographs of the Davis's home and no historical documents mention it, so all of my interpretations are drawn from archaeology and from comparing the structure to other buildings from the same time period. The home likely had a loft or attic space. The Davises raised five children. Historian Paul Schopp's research revealed that the Davises likely rented out the home after they moved closer to Rancocas Road. On April 4, 1914, William Davis died from pneumonia (Astle 2008). His government-issued gravestone is one of the eleven still standing in the Timbuctoo cemetery. There is little information about Rebecca or the Davis children, and there are no mentions of the Davis family members in the federal decennial census after 1910.

In 2009, William Chadwick and Peter Leach of John Milner and Associates completed a geophysical report that included surveys done with a magnetometer and with ground-penetrating radar (2009; see figure 3.3). These surveys were overlaid onto the historic plot maps and matched up with interpreted structures. Chadwick and Leach found features of eighteen possible dwellings and/or outbuildings, five possible shaft features, and three walkways. Each of these anomalies were tested using shovel test pits, trenches, or excavation units.

The main focus of the Timbuctoo Discovery Project's research was the Davis Site. The Davis property, which was roughly 20 feet by 100 feet, was located on what once was Haywood Street, a walkway that ran through the community. Based on the geophysical survey, Chadwick and Leach believed that the property contained a possible structure, outbuilding, and shaft feature. The Timbuctoo Discovery Project Committee came to the

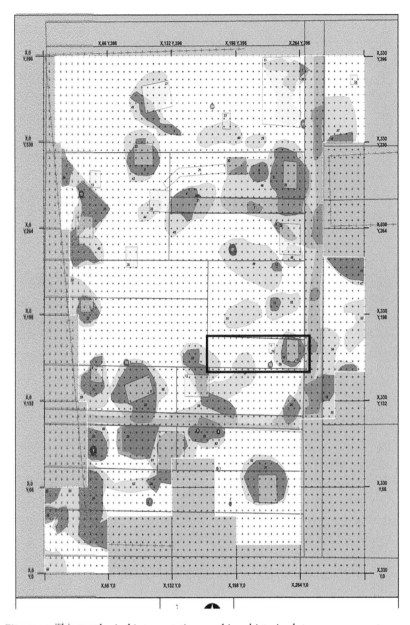

Figure 3.3. This geophysical interpretation combines historic plot maps, a magnetometer survey, and a ground-penetrating radar survey of the four acres of Timbuctoo that were held by Westampton Township during fieldwork. The dark shaded rectangle outlines the Davis lot. Based on the geophysical survey, the 20 × 100-foot lot contained a possible house foundation, an outbuilding, and a shaft feature. The Davis lot was the focus of our archaeological fieldwork. Created by William Chadwick with modifications by Christopher P. Barton. Source: Chadwick and Leach 2009.

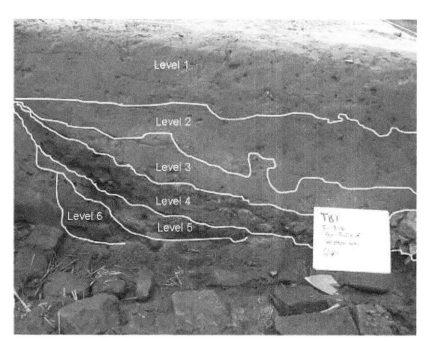

Figure 3.4. Soil profile of the community trash midden within the Davis foundation. Level 1 represents the plow zone. Levels 2 and 3 represent soil that was used to cover the midden. Levels 4, 5, and 6 represent three different deposits that created the trash midden. The majority of artifacts were recovered from Levels 4, 5, and 6. Created by Christopher P. Barton.

agreement that the Davis Site likely represented a typical homestead at the community and should be the first test area for archaeology. In October 2009, David Orr and I led a team of volunteers to shovel test the possible feature. We excavated a 2 × 2-foot shovel test pit and were able to uncover a portion of the brick foundation, identified as Feature 13.

Based on what we learned from our survey, we believe that the Davis's home was torn down and the building material was reused. The home's open foundation was used as a community trash midden until the late 1940s, when it was filled with sandy loam (see figure 3.4). In our discussions with residents and former residents, we learned that the area that is now maintained by Westampton Township had been used for farming, for raising livestock, and as a junkyard since the 1950s. The only potential reference to the Davis Site arose in a conversation with a former resident who remembered exposed bricks and debris while sledding down the hill as a child. The Davis Site and its contents were largely forgotten until our excavation.

Archaeology at the Davis Site

The Davis property was our main area of focus because both funding and time were limited. Based on interpretations from the written record, the presence of preindustrial bricks, and artifacts that date to the mid- to late nineteenth century at the base of the foundation, I believe that the Davis home was constructed in the period 1879 to the 1890s. By the turn of the twentieth century, the brickmaking industry was using machines. I believe that the structure was torn down sometime in the 1920s or 1930s, after which the foundation was used as a community trash midden. The foundation was filled with artifacts and soil as the result of anthropogenic deposits that likely were made until 1948, based on the maker's marks of several beer bottles. According to one former resident, the area that now includes the Davis lot was plowed sometime after 1950.

We recovered a total of 15,042 artifacts within and immediately outside the walls of the foundation. During our analysis, the terminus post quem, the earliest possible date for the assemblage associated with the Davis Site, is the period 1850–1869. We know this because we found fourteen fragments of a gray slipped salt-glazed stoneware jug that was manufactured in that time period. The terminus ante quem, or the date of the most recent artifact, was a porcelain tooth that we dated to around the 1950s. The majority of the artifacts recovered from the midden date from the 1910s to the 1940s (see Barton et al. 2013). However, it should be noted that the tooth was recovered from a "robber's trench" along the western wall of the brick foundation. We assigned the artifacts to one of six categories based on function (ceramics, glassware, personal/small items, faunal and floral objects, architectural objects, and miscellaneous).

Summary of Davis Site Artifact Assemblage

Ceramics constituted 17.1 percent (2,569) of the artifact assemblage. Undecorated improved whiteware was the most represented type in the ceramic assemblage. Tablewares (plates and bowls) were the most frequently identified. Our analysis of the ceramic assemblage identified a limited number of matching sets, suggesting that many of the ceramics were likely purchased piecemeal. Paul Shackel (1993, 40–41) discusses the piecemeal purchase of ceramics as a strategy marginalized people use to replace broken pieces. This practice was different from the middle-class trend of purchasing matching sets that was popular in the nineteenth and twentieth centuries. Families used matching ceramic sets to construct and project the genteel respectability of their household. However, at Timbuctoo, a lack of economic capital meant some of the residents were unable to buy tablewares in this way. They placed a greater emphasis on the function of tableware ceramics than on middle-class display.

Apart from a few pieces of medium-grade porcelain tea cups, the assemblage consists of predominantly inexpensive, low-quality ceramics, suggesting that the residents either did not have the resources to purchase more expensive wares or they simply did not want to spend money on them.

We recovered a total of 8,142 glassware artifacts (54.1 percent of the total assemblage). Datable examples ranged from the 1910s to the 1940s. Fragments of bottles and jars represented the majority of the assemblage. As I discuss in greater detail in chapter 6, one interpretation of this large percentage of glassware could be the effects of wartime rationing during both World War I and World War II. Because of the ambiguous nature of many of the glass jars, bottles, and their fragments, interpreting the contents is nearly impossible. However, we did recover several jars embossed with the words "Peanut Butter" or with images of peanuts. Peanut butter was a new, cost-effective commodified food in the early twentieth century.

Colored, molded glass tableware known as Depression glass was part of the glassware assemblage. These objects were produced from the late 1920s to the 1940s. I discuss the history and importance of Depression glass as symbolic objects in greater detail in chapter 7.

Personal items constituted 3.9 percent of the total assemblage (588 artifacts). They include clothing items and objects used for hygienic, cosmetic, or recreational purposes. A few highlights from this category include a ceramic creamer that was likely from a children's toy set, a bone toothbrush that dates from 1885 to the 1920s, and a Late Archaic jasper projectile point that dates to circa 4000–1000 BCE. The projectile point was likely redeposited in the recent past; collecting and displaying prehistoric artifacts was common in the late nineteenth century (Mullins 2001, 173–174).

A total of 691 faunal and floral remains (4.6 percent of the total assemblage) were recovered from the Davis Site. Atlantic surf clams (*Spisula solidissima*) and Eastern oysters (*Crassostrea virginica*) constituted the majority of faunal remains. Floral remains are underrepresented in the assemblage, despite the oral histories in which residents remembered enjoying tomatoes, apples, corn, plums, and peaches as children. The only plant remains recovered from the trash midden were black walnut shells (*Juglans nigra*) and one white oak acorn (*Quercus alba*), but it is unlikely that these were used as food. Cow bones constituted the majority of the livestock assemblage, although lower amounts of pig and sheep bones were also present. Machine-saw cuts on the bones suggest that the residents were purchasing inexpensive cuts of meat from a butcher. Despite scant archaeological evidence for hunting, the elders tell stories of hunting deer, pheasants, and rabbits in the woods of Timbuctoo. In the 1930s and 1940s, hunting rabbits was a tradition for children at Thanksgiving, "We used to hunt all this, years ago. And every Thanksgiving, we would all meet down [name omitted] to go hunting, and we'd say 'Well, let's go over there to get that graveyard rabbit first'" (quoted in Barton et al. 2013, 212). The fact that evidence for wildlife remains is absent could be attributable to the acid soil conditions, rodent activity, or any means of deterioration.

The architectural artifacts in the assemblage included all materials associated with construction or debris. They totaled 2,427 artifacts (15.2 percent of the total assemblage); nails constituted the majority of the assemblage. Interestingly, the percentage of shingles, wood, or other construction materials was low. This could be due to the soil conditions and subsequent deterioration or to the fact that materials from the Davis home were reused after it was torn down.

The miscellaneous category represents artifacts that did not fit into any of the other categories or were so amorphous and fragmentary that identification was impossible. A total of 815 artifacts (5.1 percent of the total assemblage) make up this portion of the assemblage. These included artifacts such as battery cells, fragments of plastic, cloth fibers, and unidentifiable fragments.

All of the archaeology at Timbuctoo reflects a community that was living in poverty. This interpretation is supported by documents and oral histories that reveal how the residents persevered throughout much of the community's history. Lack of opportunity and economic success were key reasons for the community's decline. As one descendant who still lives at Timbuctoo explains:

[Our ancestors] defaulted through lack of funds, that's what I was saying. Because most, many of the people during that period of time had very little, almost no money, and that's why many of them moved to Philadelphia. Like my family, originated from 1829, and by the time I was born, in Philadelphia, that is, in '36, well after that period of time, everybody went to Philadelphia for work, because that's the only way they could sustain. (quoted in Barton et al. 2013, 147)

While many residents moved away in search of economic opportunities, others stayed at Timbuctoo as the community declined. Several of the current residents can trace their ancestry at Timbuctoo back to the founding of the community in the 1820s. Their stories, like those of the former residents who still visit, feature family struggles and pain. They also speak of a community's perseverance and triumph.

4

LANDSCAPES OF TIMBUCTOO

The built environment offers archaeologists a unique way to understand past people in ways that go beyond excavation units and shovel test pits. In this chapter, I focus on landscape archaeology at Timbuctoo. I first look at the settlement pattern of the community and then at the practice of yard sweeping at the Davis Site. These two practices have deep roots for the people of the African Diaspora and serve both functional and social purposes for impoverished people.

The Layout of the Community

Historical records suggest that the core portion of Timbuctoo was closer to the creek than to the road. That area is where the Timbuctoo Discovery Project focused our research. Rancocas Road, which ran along the northern boundary of Timbuctoo, also connected the community to Mount Holly and other communities.

The geophysical survey of the four acres owned by Westampton Township offered us valuable clues about the potential below-ground features at Timbuctoo (Chadwick and Leach 2009). The first thing we noticed about these data were how the interpreted structures, possible dwellings or outbuildings (represented in figure 4.2 as squares), correlated directly with the historic plot map. The survey indicated that each structure was situated in its lot as indicated on the plot map. The geophysical survey and our shovel testing also suggested that there were no fences or other physical barriers between the properties. In our field survey, we ground tested four of the interpreted structures with shovel testing and trenches (Barton et al. 2013). This methodology, which was developed in collaboration with the Timbuctoo Discovery Project and Westampton Township, protected the site from archaeological disturbance and focused our limited resources on the Davis

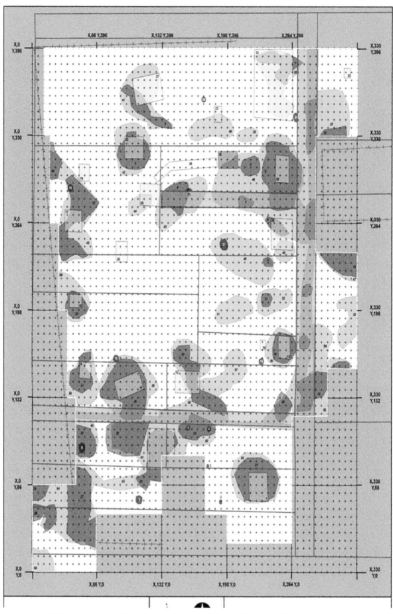

Figure 4.1. This geophysical interpretation combines historic plot maps, a magnetometer survey, and a ground-penetrating radar survey of the four acres of Timbuctoo that was held by Westampton Township during fieldwork. The seventeen shaded squares represent possible house or outbuilding foundations. The three medium-shaded rectangles represent historic pathways; including what once was Haywood Street to the east. Created by William Chadwick. Source: Chadwick and Leach 2009.

Site. Our analysis of the recovered artifacts, which included ceramics and bottle glass, indicated that the sites were all from the mid-nineteenth to the early twentieth centuries (Barton 2013).

The second thing that we saw in the geophysical survey was the circular settlement pattern of Timbuctoo. It featured an open area in the center that did not yield any data from the magnetometer or from ground-penetrating radar. When we did shovel testing in this center, we did not recover any artifacts that date to the period. The absence of artifacts was interesting, given that both census records and the geophysical survey suggest that this four-acre area was inhabited for some time. Soil profile analyses suggested that the area had been plowed in the recent past, and there was evidence for a buried occupation level at the same depth of 0.9 to 1.0 feet (Barton 2013; Barton et al. 2013).

For archaeologists, the absence of things and features—the space between places—can be as telling as recovery and discovery (Yentsch 1994, xxvii). The open space suggested to us that the core area may have been used in a communal way. Historical sources document that Timbuctoo hosted several camp meetings, or outdoor spiritual revival meetings, in the latter half of the nineteenth century. Some white neighbors joined the residents of Timbuctoo at these meetings.[1] Camp meetings were very popular. In September 1887, the *Morning Post* offered this report:

> The colored camp meeting at Timbuctoo will be continued till Monday, Sept. 6th. Rev. W. H. Wayman pastor in charge. The meeting has been a grand success, some 4,000 people being on the ground last Sunday, and a larger party is looked for on Sunday, the 5th.[2]

The exact locations of these camp meetings are unknown, but the open space, which is located between the houses and near the church, could have served as a gathering site. In the first half of the nineteenth century, Timbuctoo residents had community celebrations on Sundays and on holidays. One elder reported that "when the church use to [be] down there, they'd have big gatherings, and underneath of them big trees there, across from the cemetery, and we'd put up tables and white tablecloths and things" (quoted in Barton et al. 2013). These community events illustrate the importance of the landscape in fostering and maintaining a collective identity at Timbuctoo.

Parting Ways, a Black settlement in Plymouth, Massachusetts, had a similar settlement pattern. The community was founded by four formerly enslaved men and their families after the men served in the American

Revolution. James Deetz (1996) discussed several African-inspired practices that families at Parting Ways followed, including architecture, how they prepared their food, and settlement patterns. The four families collectively owned 94 contiguous acres of land as individual farms, and they built their homes at the center of the site. Deetz notes that this settlement pattern contrasts with the Anglo-American tradition in which an individual landowner places their home on their own property, apart from others. This Anglo-American practice reflected an ideology of individualism, a worldview that socialized people to see themselves as unique and apart from others. Deetz suggests that at Parting Ways, the settlement pattern emphasized a collective identity that valued how the families offered each other assistance and reassurance.

The settlement pattern at Timbuctoo is evidence of a similar collective identity and ethic of mutual assistance. Whether this view of the landscape was rooted in a West African belief system is not clear from the available evidence, but the site's history and the experiences of the residents are clear evidence of a collective identity that differed from that of nearby white households. The absence of fencing or physical boundaries between properties on the four acres is evidence of a community that looked out for each other. Life on the lower end of the economic spectrum meant that many parents had to work long hours or even take on multiple jobs in order to feed their families. Mutual assistance came in many forms, including financial help, food support, and child care. As one elder noted about Timbuctoo in the 1930s and 1940s, "It was a nice village then, we all got along. All of them had big families. My mother was a midwife, and when anyone had to have a baby, then she would deliver it. . . . So they all took care of each other, all looked out for each other, and if you all got in trouble, the other one would know about it." This is similar to what researchers have found in other marginalized communities (Geismar 1982; Matthews 2020; Wall 1999; Saitta 2007).

The community lived the African proverb that "it takes a village to raise a child." The elders tell stories of how parents watched each other's children and reported back if a child misbehaved (Barton et al. 2013, 152). One elder says that after getting in trouble, "you'd get home, your mother be waiting for you. They must've had smoke, back then they didn't have telephones, they must've had smoke signals or something. By the time you got home, boy, your father or your mother waiting for you with a belt or a switch." Communal help in the rearing of children is common among impoverished communities (Stack 2008, 43–46; Wall 1991, 79).

The extant written records and the oral histories document how the people of the community identified themselves as being from "Bucktoe," members of a community that not only lived in the defined area but also shared an economic and social marginalized status. This internalized worldview of "us" and "them" regarded Timbuctoo as unique and separate from the outside world. The community's experiences with slave catchers in the nineteenth century and the Ku Klux Klan in the twentieth century provide examples of mutual assistance. As discussed in chapter 3, when Perry Simmons was besieged by slave catchers, the community quickly assembled and came to his aid. Even though it appears that Simmons did not live in the four acres that we focused on archaeologically, community members were able to spread the word and come to his aid. Similarly, the incident of the confrontation that almost happened between the residents and the KKK following a schoolyard fight between two children in the mid-twentieth century shows evidence of mutual assistance and support. The ability of the residents to be alerted to danger reflects a collective identity and collective action at Timbuctoo.

Yard Sweeping

The collective identity at Timbuctoo can also be seen in the swept yards of the community. A yard is a physical and mental extension of the household (Jenkins 1994; Gundaker and McWillie 2004; Battle-Baptiste 2010, 2011). Barbara Heath and Amber Bennett (2000, 38) characterize a yard as the area that immediately surrounds a house as an area for performing everyday activities. These can include food processing or preparation, animal care, work tasks, play, and socializing. They explain that the ambiguity of their definition is intentional in order to incorporate spatial, temporal, sociocultural, and regional differences in yard use and yet still facilitate a general understanding of what constitutes a yard.

The Davis Lot

Our excavation of the Davis home revealed a noticeable absence of artifacts (n = 276, 0.01 percent of the total assemblage) from outside the foundation at the interpreted occupation (level 3). Additionally, all of the 276 fragmented artifacts collected were located less than 1.5 feet outside the foundation wall and were present only in Units 4 and 6. This pattern of artifact scattering was likely the result of repeated plowing that redistributed the

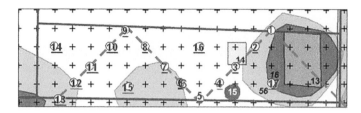

Figure 4.2. Sample testing of the Davis lot. Source: Chadwick and Leach 2009, with modifications by Christopher P. Barton.

fragments. No other artifacts were recovered from any other excavation units surrounding the perimeter of the house foundation at or below the occupation level. Given the site's history, the ancestry of the residents, and the absence of artifacts in the area immediately around the home, I believed that we uncovered evidence for yard sweeping. I developed four criteria and reviewed the wealth of archaeological literature relating to swept yards on Black-occupied sites to support this interpretation.

Methodology

We used four criteria to investigate the possibility of yard sweeping at the Davis Site in Timbuctoo. First, we consulted the local United States Department of Agriculture soil survey for the site (United States Department of Agriculture 2011). The survey reports that Collington fine sandy loam is the primary soil composition for the Davis lot. Collington is often found on knobs and hill slopes. However, during our excavations and shovel testing, we encountered two different stratigraphic levels. Level 1 (Munsell 10 YR 4/4; dark yellowish brown, sandy loam) is located roughly 1 foot below contemporary grade. Level 2 (Munsell 10 YR 5/4; yellowish brown, sandy clay loam) is roughly 1 to 3.5 feet below contemporary grade (see figure 4.3). This uniformity likely represented a plow zone, as there was no evidence that the area had been stripped of topsoil in the recent past. An elder remembered the plateau being used for small-scale farming. They also remembered fragments of exposed brick near the Davis Site when they were sledding there in childhood (Barton et al. 2013).

The second criterion is the absence of humus and/or a darkened buried layer at the interpreted occupation level of the site. While the Davis home is on top of a small plateau, the lot was separated from the talus slope by a small dirt pathway on the eastern side of the village that once was called Haywood Street. Any alluvial, colluvial, and/or aeolian redistribution of

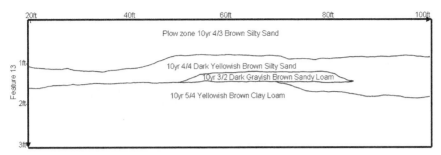

Figure 4.3. The interpreted soil profile of the Davis lot. The 10 YR 3/2 Dark Grayish Brown layer is interpreted as the end of Davis's swept yard. This scatter layer contained evidence for vegetation and artifact fragments. Created by Christopher P. Barton.

artifacts from the Davis home or lot by water or gravity would have placed them within the areas we tested. During our excavation, we noted that there was no evidence for humus and/or a buried darkened layer at the interpreted occupation level. Archaeologists often look for dark or discolored levels below the modern surface. These levels, or strata, often become dark because the level above them either had vegetation or collected water for a period of time. As the level is exposed, the organic material from the vegetation or the filtering of water causes a leaching of minerals that darkens the stratum. These darkened strata are important because if the level was exposed long enough to have vegetation grow in it, then it could have been occupied by humans at one time. Some archaeologists refer to this as a "buried A horizon." However, at the Davis site we did not see such a level at what we had interpreted as the occupation level. This suggested to us that the area immediately around the Davis house had little or no vegetation as a result of erosion and/or regular sweeping.

Third, apart from a few ferrous metal fragments that were likely kicked up from repeated plowing, we noticed an absence of artifacts outside the foundation of the house during our excavations. Given the small size of the home, the fact that seven people lived in it, and the heat of New Jersey summers, I believe that the yard was used as an extension of the home. The use of the immediate outdoor space of a home for socializing and work has been well documented at Black sites in the United States (e.g., Gall et al. 2020, 316; Battle-Baptiste 2010; Gundaker and McWillie 2004; Heath and Bennett 2000; Cabak et al. 1999, 29).

The fourth criterion of our research centered on the historical practice of yard sweeping by Black people and economically marginalized groups in the United States. This information provided context for our interpretation.

Using these four criteria, we developed a conservative testing plan that would enable us to recover data from the yard space but also preserve the Davis house lot. We did a systematic survey of the 20 × 100-foot lot at staggered six-foot intervals using a hand auger and split spoons. We measured the boring depths of our sample from the southwestern datum point of excavation Unit 9. There was a less than 2 percent slope from that datum point to the western property line of the Davis lot. The combination of this sample testing and the 18 × 18-foot excavation of the Davis house accounted for 327 square feet (1.6 percent) of the total 2,000 square feet of the Davis Site. We created this conservative sample to limit destruction of the site.

Our survey findings, specifically Borings 1, 2, 3, and 17, showed a pattern of compacted clay loam with no recovered artifacts, similar to what we observed in our excavations immediately around the foundations of the home. However, with Borings 4, 5, and 16, each of which was less than 24 feet from Feature 13, we saw a very thin (< 0.05 feet), dark-grayish-brown stratum that appeared in the profile at roughly 1 foot below contemporary grade. At a depth that we believed represented the occupation level, the stratum grew to a maximum thickness of 0.06 feet in Borings 6, 7, 8, 9, 10, 11, 14, and 15 as we tested farther away from the Davis home. We recovered small fragments of charcoal, bricks, glass, transfer-printed ironstone, and unidentifiable metal from this buried surface level. This pattern of artifact scatter is common for yard sweeping; the scatter is often found along property lines or away from places of social interaction. A person sweeping a yard does not remove the debris completely but rather moves the objects away from the immediate vicinity of the structure (Orser 1988, 135). We found artifact fragments in Borings 6, 7, 8, 9, 10, 11, 14, and 15 at locations that were closest to the property line and farthest away from the Davis home (see figure 4.2). Interestingly, the buried surface disappeared during our testing at Boring 13 at a depth of 1.1 feet (less than 6 feet from the southwest corner of the Davis lot). The geophysical survey and our shovel testing revealed that this area was near another foundation, that of the home of Charles Henry Love, a retired USCT soldier of the 22nd Regiment. Unfortunately, we were unable to contact the lot's owner and were not able to excavate the Love site. However, our shovel test pit and borings near the property line showed artifacts similar to what we found around the Davis home and a similar absence of a buried A horizon. These data suggest that someone at the Love household swept the area to the east of the home, as was the case at the Davis household. Our testing indicates that someone in that family regularly swept at least 24 feet around the Davis home (see figure 4.3).

The area beyond this 24-foot boundary shows evidence of a buried level where there was some vegetation at one time. Unfortunately, we do not have photographs from the era and the elders did not mention yard sweeping, but the African-inspired practice had gone out of fashion by the turn of the twentieth century.

Archaeologies of Yard Sweeping

Because we did not see the brush strokes or bristle scars in our archaeological excavations, my interpretation that the yard was swept required context. Historical and ethnographic accounts of Black yard sweeping provide information about the possible origins, meanings, and significance of swept yards. These accounts of sweeping within Black communities trace the practice to spiritual and ceremonial rituals for moving malevolent spirits away from the home (MacGaffey 1986; Heath and Bennett 2000; Gundaker and McWillie 2004). People of African descent in the United States have been practicing yard sweeping since colonial times, although the meanings and significance have changed over time and differ by location. Most archaeological observations of Black swept yards have been in the southeastern United States, though evidence has been observed as far north as the African Meeting House in Nantucket, Massachusetts (Beaudry and Berkland 2007, 405).

This evidence for sweeping underscores the heterogeneity of the practice. Whitney Battle-Baptiste (2010, 2011) analyzes Black yard sweeping in the context of race, class, gender, identity, and resistance. She focuses on the landscape at the quarters at the First Hermitage in Tennessee as evidence of the social networks of enslaved black women in the nineteenth century. She argues that sweeping was rooted within West African spiritualism and discusses how the practice and its meanings changed over time and space. As extensions of the home, swept yards were shaped landscapes that were imbued with collective significance and meaning. Swept yards were not just stages for religious ceremonies, they were also arenas for work and for the socializing people did while they did laundry, prepared food, and minded children. Battle-Baptiste argues that creating and maintaining swept yards sustained Black resistance because it provided a space for vital social interaction. She contends that at the First Hermitage, where the owner and enslaved people lived less than 40 feet from one another, swept yards created a clear separation between the outside world of human bondage and the private sphere that enslaved women cultivated and controlled. She argues that women swept yards "to protect against master and the undesirable spirits of the plantation. . . . [The sweeper] is protecting her home, her family, her community by creating a spiritual boundary that is recognized by her people. These actions were performed by women, the methods passed down from woman to woman, generation to generation" (Battle-Baptiste 2010, 89).

This historical context suggests that swept yards were stages for socializing the five Davis children into a collective Black identity. Battle-Baptiste (2011, 100) underscores that during slavery, while the swept yard was used during the day for tasks that planters often dictated to enslaved peoples, the yard became a sacred, personal place for families at night. The swept surfaces of the yards that surrounded the homes of enslaved peoples were cultivated social landscapes where they formed collective identities, memories, and individual practices.

In her review of historical archaeology in Delaware, LuAnn De Cunzo (2004, 245–247) also interpreted evidence of Black yard sweeping as a practice rooted in West African traditions. De Cunzo identifies four ways that Black people used yards. First, swept yards offered spiritual protection for the home's inhabitants. As the person swept any physical debris away from the home, they were also creating a sacred space by sweeping away any malicious spirits. Second, the cleaned surface areas of the yard underscored the virtue of the owner. For people who were socialized into the practice, the clean exposed soil showed that the individual adhered to social norms about respectability. Third, the cleaned surfaces on which daily tasks and socializing occurred projected the identity of the individual, and by extension, the collective identity of the community. De Cunzo (2004, 234) also states that the maintained area of the yard was a sacred place for honoring the individual's family and ancestors. The yard reflected the present owner's identity and their remembrance of their ancestral ties. For De Cunzo (2004, 234), these four purposes constitute a unique Black worldview. Swept yards helped link people to place through a shared collective identity that emphasized belonging and tradition. This expression of collective identity contrasted with the white middle-class practice of fencing in lawns and flower gardens in the late nineteenth century. The rise of lawns on middle-class properties is attributable to three factors: the popularity of landscaping literature, the mass production of landscaping tools (particularly the lawn mower), and the growth of the suburbs in the Northeast.

In an effort to situate yard sweeping at Timbuctoo in its historical context, I compared the practice with discussions of middle-class yards in late-nineteenth- and early twentieth-century landscaping manuals. This literature, which was popular when it was published, can help us understand the white middle-class public's view of landscapes.

Landscaping manuals told readers how to create and maintain manicured landscapes and lawns (Jonsson-Rose 1897; Jenkins 1994). The upper classes used gardens and lawns to underscore their economic and social capital (Leone 1984; Chesney 2014). These forms of material culture projected the economic wealth and taste of the individual and their scientific knowledge of horticulture. As Mark Leone (1984) notes, in the absence of an aristocracy in the early United States, members of the upper class used wealth and knowledge to emphasize their elite status. They did so to create the illusion of a noble class that was defined by capitalism rather than bloodlines and titles. In the late nineteenth century, members of the suburban middle class sought to project respectability by emulating how wealthy people crafted their lawns and gardens (Jenkins 1994, 21–33). In *Lawns and Gardens: How to Plant and Beautify the Home Lot, the Pleasure Ground, and Garden* (1897), Nils Jonsson-Rose explained why lawns and gardens were important:

> To a great extent the character and beauty of a garden depends on a lawn. A level lawn gives an impression of peace and quiet; an undulating one wears an expression of cheerfulness. Gardens with well-trimmed, close and velvety lawns are beautiful and attractive. . . . But when the lawn adopts the choicest flowers of the field and meadow, and shrubberies and thickets are filled with woodland blossoms, then the garden becomes, as far as our impressions are concerned, a part of nature itself. (1897, 112–113)

Colorful flowerbeds, trimmed hedges, and lush green lawns were powerful markers that conveyed the owner's individuality and their genteel middle-class identity. These maintained areas were socially and physically constructed spaces that owners presented as an extension of the home. However, the meanings and functions of the lawns and flower gardens of the white middle class contrasted with those of the swept yards at Timbuctoo.

In the nineteenth century, the yard of a white middle-class home was a domestic space that was individualized and compartmentalized through fences that created boundaries between the household and the outside world. James Deetz (1996) discusses how settlement patterns reflected shifts in ideology from collectivism to individualism in colonial New England. In contrast to the early colonial pattern of densely clustered villages surrounded by farmlands, by the late eighteenth century, the pattern had shifted to semi-isolated households marked by fences that clearly delineated the personal property of the individual. A fenced-in home, a lush lawn, and a flower garden created a display that conveyed that the house and its inhabitants were well ordered and respectable. Peter Henderson (1887, 22–23) described the new attitude of the white middle class in the late nineteenth century:

> Since the introduction of the lawn-mowers, the keeping of the lawn has been so simplified that no suburban residence is complete without one, and there [are] now no more excuses for tall grass "going to hay" in the door than there would be for cobwebs taking possession of the rooms inside the dwelling. We occasionally see some parsimonious individual, even now, who remembers that in his grandfather's days, grass was allowed to grow for the food of the "critters," and he leaves it for food for his "critters" still. Though at the same time his furniture inside, that nobody but himself ever sees, or has an opportunity to admire, for such men are not troubled with friends, may have cost him $5,000 or $10,000. We have two or three notable examples of this kind in my immediate neighborhood, but it is gratifying to know that such neighbors are not numerous, for the example of the majority will soon shame them into decency.

The second reason for the rise in popularity of lawns was the mass production of lawn mowers. In the context of the new middle-class norm of respectability, the availability of lawn mowers meant that a person's failure to maintain their lawn also indicated a failure to adhere to cultural norms. As was the case in the Henderson quote, people who failed to adapt to the new norm risked being ostracized by their neighbors. Henderson declared it did not matter how wealthy a person was, if their yard was unkempt, their home was offensive, as were they themselves. This is an extreme view that likely did not represent the norm, but it does offer an interesting insight into how well-kept lawns and gardens were viewed as signifiers of an individual's identity and their willingness to conform to middle-class trends in landscaping as a way of signaling respectability.

This new social norm regarding the areas around the household contrasted with swept yards in several ways. Etiquette books argued that while middle-class children could use the lawn for play, it was not to be used by adults. Adults were to socialize with their peers inside the home, in the parlor (Mullins 2001). These networks of capitalism and consumer culture placed an importance on economic and symbolic capitals; the parlor and the objects displayed there were the focal points of the household. Hosts would serve tea and discuss the issues of the day in rooms filled with bric-a-brac and trinkets. The parlor expressed an individual's respectability and middle-class gentility. The lawn projected the same status and identities as the parlor, but it did not have the same functional use as a space for socializing. All of this was made possible by the growth of the suburbs in the Northeast. The suburbs represented homeownership and a return to nature (Herman et al. 1990, 5), and the yard was central to both of these goals. But while the tradition of swept yards persisted in the South, in the suburbs of the Northeast, a person's yard was supposed to have a lawn (Jenkins 1994, 4). These northeastern, middle-class manicured yards were to be looked at and admired by onlookers but were not to be used as physical extensions of the household. The rise of suburbs outside Boston, Philadelphia, and New York not only transformed the physical landscape; with the rise of social etiquette literature and the mass production of lawn equipment, they also altered the ways people viewed their immediate surroundings. Black people in the South continued the practice of yard sweeping, as did some impoverished white communities in the South, where middle-class suburbs didn't emerge until the mid-twentieth century (Jenkins 1994).

Researchers have often interpreted the swept yards of white people as a functional response to the pressures of economic class (Gundaker and McWillie 2004, 112). In her study of the homes of predominantly Irish and Irish Americans who worked at Squirrel Run, a gunpowder factory and workers' village in northern Delaware, in the late nineteenth century, Margaret Mulrooney (2002) discusses how the workers' yards were multipurpose spaces used for work, cooking, raising livestock, and socializing. She writes, "Grass did not grow well under the heavy foot traffic, but flagstones, broken shells, and board provided firm footing on rainy days" (Mulrooney 2002, 168–169). But it was likely not just the foot traffic that kept the area free from grass; as Mulrooney notes, the workers did not like having any debris in their yards.

At nearby Blacksmith's Hill, Delaware, archaeologist Samuel Shogren (1986) led a survey of workers' housing and a communal trash pit. Shogren suggests that residents swept trash from their yards into the pit to keep work areas tidy. Members of the working class, for whom the boundaries of work and home were blurred, needed a clean yard surface where they could perform work tasks and socialize.

Another reason for bare swept yards, particularly in the South, was that they deterred insects, pests, and snakes (Jenkins 1994, 15; Gundaker and McWillie 2004, 111). The practice was still used in the late twentieth century, as a mid-1990s letter to the *New York Times* from Ray Berry, who grew up in the Lowcountry of South Carolina, indicates. Berry remembered that both white and black people swept yards in South Carolina:

> I remember my paternal grandmother telling me that my white ancestors also swept yards every morning at daybreak in the early years of the century. There is one reason this tradition exists—remember, it is quite labor-intensive—and it has nothing with the looks of the yard and garden. . . . It is solely about the tracks of poisonous snakes.[3]

Reflecting on his childhood in the Lowcountry of South Carolina, the author not only touches upon the practical uses of sweeping to keep snakes away from the home, he also discusses the practice among his white ancestors. Yard sweeping in the South transcended the color line among impoverished Black and white people. The small dwellings of impoverished people in the South were often unbearably hot in the summer months, and swept and shaded yards were areas where people could get some relief from the heat (Gundaker and McWillie 2004, 111). The 12 × 16-foot dwelling at the Davis Site was likely something like a sweatbox in the summer. Moreover, because the home's interior space was small, doing laundry and mingling with family and friends likely took place in the swept yard. Yard sweeping is a practice that is transmitted from generation to generation (Battle-Baptiste 2011, 100), and while the origins of Timbuctoo's swept yards may be West African, it was also a reflection of economic class.

For people socialized in the practice of yard sweeping, yards were not inanimate stages; they were dynamic landscapes. While swept surfaces were devoid of plant life, they were not devoid of everyday life. Yards were areas where people learned, worked, and socialized in a welcoming extension of home. People came together, not apart, on the bare grounds of swept yards. The social and economic realities of impoverished people like the Davises prevented them from building large homes with high vaulted ceilings where they could escape the heat, keep out pests, and socialize in a cool indoor area. The yard provided a multipurpose area where people could engage in a wide array of practices. The swept yard was much more than simply a functional response to poverty: it embodied the collective identity of the Timbuctoo community.

5

THE DAVIS HOME

In 1879, William Davis purchased a 20 × 100-foot lot from the estate of Mary Simmons. The Davis family constructed their home on this lot on a 12 × 16-foot foundation (192 square feet). The foundation consisted of four sides of running brick perimeter that was one course thick with corner piers that were up to three courses thick. The foundation was dry laid, but some residual sand-based mortar can be seen on several recovered bricks. This suggests that they may have been taken from another structure and re-used in the foundation of the Davis house. Recycling and reusing construction materials is a common practice among marginalized people (Wilkie 2000, 153–154; Ponansky 2004, 41; Barnes 2011). On the eastern wall, the brick foundation is twelve courses high, the maximum height. Evidence of plow scars and brick fragments in excavation levels 1 and 2 suggests that the uppermost portion of the foundation was likely higher than its current grade. Although the interior of the foundation was eventually used as a community trash midden, only a small amount of architectural debris was recovered from that part of the site, suggesting that the dwelling was demolished and materials were removed. Without direct evidence apart from the foundation, interpreting the architecture of the home involves speculation. However, comparable historical photos of dwellings near Timbuctoo suggest that the home was likely a one-story design (with a possible loft) that rested on four corner piers.

Figure 5.1 depicts a one-room dwelling built on piers. This photo of a farmworker and his home in Burlington County, New Jersey, was taken in 1938. The balloon-framed house of this farmworker is supported by baseboards positioned on brick piers. The exterior is likely clapboard covered with a fabric wrapping to protect the interior from weather. The one-room

Figure 5.1. A Farm Security Administration photograph of an agricultural worker in a one-room shack in Burlington County, New Jersey, in 1938. Library of Congress, Prints & Photographs Division, https://www.loc.gov/item/2017776941. Photo by Arthur Rothstein.

home has a slightly pitched roof with a protruding chimney stack. The yard was compacted and appears to have been swept. Although the one-room house was smaller than the Davis home, its owner and the Davises were living in poverty that caused them to use similar construction methods and materials.

Figure 5.2 is another example of a home that may have been similar to the Davis home. Entitled "Negro Shack," this image was taken in New Jersey by Carl Mydans of the Resettlement Administration in 1935. The home rested on a foundation of running brick. The balloon-framed house has clapboard on the exterior. The sills, framing, and panes of the three visible windows do not match. This suggests that either the windows were replaced at different times or were bought individually. The gabled roof supports a brick chimney, although the angle of the photograph makes it difficult to determine its exact location. The yard is difficult to see because of a layer of snow, but there is little evidence of vegetation around the entrance and side of the house. Based on the estimated height of the woman in the doorway, we believe that this house was close to the size of the Davis house.

Figure 5.2. "Negro shack," New Jersey, 1935. Photo by Carl Mydans. Courtesy of New York Public Library, Resettlement Administration Photographs Collection.

Although the Davises purchased their 20 × 100-foot lot in 1879, the construction methods and materials they used had not changed much for impoverished people by the 1930s. In our excavations outside the foundation walls we noticed no evidence of a builder's trench. In a construction process that uses a builder's trench, the soil is dug out, the four foundation walls are laid, and the center soil remains undisturbed. When this method is used, the soil used to fill in around the foundation never becomes as compacted as the virgin soil in the center. Through our analysis of soil profiles and soil discoloration and simply by feeling the difference in the soils we noticed that in the area outside the brick foundation, the soil was undisturbed and compact. This suggests that a builder's trench was not used. We believe that the builders of the Davis home created a large excavation that was big enough for their needs and then placed the foundation directly against the undisturbed clay loam for support. As discussed in chapter 4, one avenue for our research has been comparing the practices at Timbuctoo to popular trends in landscaping. At the Davis site, we focused on comparing building practices and materials used with building practices that were common at the time the house was built. According to turn-of-the-century trade manuals, the methods Davis used were common practices for the era (Brown 1885, 107–108). However, this method of supporting the foundation walls by undisturbed soil was not recommended for excavations in clay soils like those at Timbuctoo. Clark (1895, 108) wrote that

> clayey soils are also unfavorable [for foundation excavation]. Being impervious, they retain the water which may settle into the new excavation, just outside the cellar walls, until it finds an escape for itself, very probably into the building. Moreover, they expand greatly in wet seasons, or in frosty weather, to contract again in summers; while the tenacity with which frozen clay clings to stone or brick work often causes dislocation or derangement of cellar walls and piers.

For many people like Davis, limited money, time, and access to materials restricted the practices and resources they used to construct their homes. People living at or below the poverty line were either unable to follow or rejected popular trends in architecture. Military pension and census records suggest that Davis had limited resources for building a home.

In an effort to conserve the foundation, we left the majority of bricks in situ (figure 5.3). However, we recovered and cataloged thirteen complete bricks from the site. They were handmade from a soft mud mixture. All of the bricks were poorly molded and had porous bodies and soft edges. During the manufacturing process the surfaces of the brick were struck with sand, which left them rough and gritty. Most of the bricks in the foundation are either salmon colored or are semi-vitrified (figure 5.4). Salmon bricks are pink in color and are less dense than properly fired bricks because they are baked at a distance from the heat source. Semi-vitrified bricks are baked closer to the heat source and become "burned" on one end. This causes the sand and silica to melt, creating a black, sometimes glazed, look to the exterior. These types of bricks are often smaller than properly fired brick because of this "melting." Consequently, the poor aesthetics and quality meant that builders often cast away salmon and semi-vitrified bricks.

All of the recovered bricks from Timbuctoo were unevenly fired, resulting in a range of densities. Variations in the color, density, and size of the brick could be the result of several interrelated factors. First, it could be the case that the bricks were taken from different stocks. Second, brick traits can be influenced by the characteristics of the mold that was used to make them (Lynch 1994, 74). Third, certain characteristics of the clay and/or additives to the mix may cause variations. Fourth, the handling and

Left: Figure 5.3. Eastern view of the foundation of the Davis home. Photo by Christopher P. Barton.

Below: Figure 5.4. Photo of the brick foundation of the Davis home that was used as a community trash midden until the 1940s. The three shovel test pits in the center were used to confirm that there were no artifacts below the foundation level. During excavation we left the eastern and western walls intact in order to persevere the integrity of the foundation. Photo by Christopher P. Barton.

processing of "green" bricks can affect the color, density, and size. Fifth, the proximity of the bricks to the heat source during firing will greatly influence the physical traits of the brick (Gurcke 1987, 116). Finally, if improperly fired bricks are set in poorly drained soils, like those of the Davis Site, their physical composition can be affected over time. We believe that the variation in the bricks of the Davis home indicates that they were fired at a nearby brickyard, they were fired in a scove kiln, or they were burned in a wet clamp at Timbuctoo.[1]

Using scove kilns to fire bricks was a common practice at the turn of the century. Ries, Kummel, and Knapp (1904, 240) described an updraft scove kiln:

> The [green] bricks are set in large rectangular masses from 38 to 54 courses high, depending on the kind of clay. In building up the mass a series of parallel arches is left running through the mass from side to side, and with their centers about two feet apart. After the bricks are set up they are surrounded by a wall two courses deep of "double-coal" brick, and the whole outside of the mass daubed with wet clay to prevent the entrance of cold air during burning. The top of the kiln is then closed by a layer of bricks laid close together and termed platting.

Two brickyards were operating near Timbuctoo in the late nineteenth and early twentieth centuries. Several Timbuctoo residents, including William Davis, were employed at these brickyards. In 1904, Ries, Kummel, and Knapp described the clay and the brickyards in the area:

> Clay Marl IV, or a surface clay derived from it, is worked at two localities in Burlington County. It is dug in two clay pits just north of Timbuctoo . . . and 1 1/2 miles northwest of Northampton, and supplies two small brickyards. When molded by hand and burned in scove kilns, it makes a porous brick. Harder burning would improve it. (387)

It was hard to control the temperature inside a scove kiln, and such kilns could not reach high temperatures. They were used to make "common" bricks rather than fire, face, or other specialty bricks (Ries, Kummel, and Knapp 1904, 204–205). The products of scove kilns ranged in quality and included salmon and semi-vitrified bricks.

I wanted to better understand how the bricks we recovered would have been viewed according to the standards of contemporary builders.

For example, in 1885, Brown wrote in *Healthy Foundations for Houses* that scove kilns produced a quality of bricks that was not recommended for foundations:

> Bricks are usually found in three conditions as to hardness. Arch brick, as they form the arch in the kiln, come in direct contact with the fire. These bricks are hard, generally slightly vitrified or glazed, but they are usually distorted. When well-shaped these arch bricks make the best foundations. The bricks farthest from the fire (Salmon) are imperfectly burned, and are worthless for foundations, as they absorb water and disintegrate easily. The medium bricks may be used when they are well burned. . . . Usually in this country light red or "salmon bricks" are inferior and unfit for foundations; dark red bricks are good and may be used in foundations, while bluish or greenish bricks are vitrified, and, if properly shaped, make the best foundations. (Brown 1885, 105–106)

The inconsistent quality of bricks burned in a scove kiln meant that 20–30 percent of the lot was rejected for sale, reused to build the next scove kiln, or crushed and used in new mix (Gurcke 1987, 32; Lynch 1994, 4). Trade manuals advised customers to reject "all bad shaped and unsound bricks. Good bricks are regular in shape, with plane surfaces and sharp, true angles" (Powell 1879, 29). However, the bricks at Timbuctoo lack smooth surfaces and straight edges and corners. They are rough, they have soft edges, and their size varies.

Another possible reason for the variations in the Davis bricks is that they may have been burned using an onsite wet clamp. Wet clamps have been used for millennia. Their use did not decline until the 1870s, with the rise of machines to make bricks (Lynch 1994, 22). Constructing a wet clamp required a considerable amount of time, skill, and labor. Brickmaking was often a family occupation. "The father worked as the molder and was served by his family, usually in gangs of six. Each had a specific job: mixing, carrying clay, fetching, molding, or hacking" (Lynch 1994, 78). Given that William Davis was a brick molder before he enlisted in the USCT, he may have been able to make bricks or at least instruct others about the process. The theory that the source of the Davis bricks may have been an onsite wet clamp is based on our knowledge of William Davis's experience and the similarities of the foundation bricks with bricks produced in wet clamps (Gurcke 1987, 32). However, determining the exact source of the bricks is outside the scope of this chapter. We focused on understanding how the quality of the bricks at the Davis site compared to building standards at the turn of the twentieth century.

Scove kilns and wet clamps often created improperly burned bricks that professional builders would not use because of popular trends in home construction. In the early to mid-nineteenth century, bricklayers used inexpensive common bricks on exteriors and covered over them with stucco to hide the brick face (Lynch 1994, 54). In the 1870s, brick facades became popular; bricklayers used "face bricks" on exteriors instead of using the more uniform common brick (Lynch 1994, 15). The appearance of face bricks in buildings coincided with the rise of machine manufacturing. Mechanized wire cutting and machine press molding resulted in more uniform sizes, colors, textures, and densities. Machines gave brickmakers much more control over the manufacturing process and decreased the percentage of unusable product (Lynch 1994, 22). These advances put stress on yards that used traditional handmade bricks, like those near Timbuctoo. Most of the cost of handmade bricks was allocated to labor, and the traditional practice could not meet mass production standards or popular tastes for uniformity. Furthermore, while some architects used handmade rough-surfaced bricks in an aesthetic niche market, by the late nineteenth century their use in general home construction had declined significantly (Lynch 1994, 61). This transition in popular architectural trends meant that common, handmade bricks were used only in foundations and underground sewers and as insulation known as nogging (Sayre & Fisher Co. 1895, 117). In *A Practical Treatise on Brick, Tiles and Terra-Cotta* (1885), Charles Davis stated that some rough-surfaced bricks, like those of the Davis foundation, were known as "washers" and were used specifically for foundation work.

> If there should be indication of rain before the usual time for "taking in of the brick," and any of the brick are hard enough to handle, they are wheeled into the shed; if not firm enough, they are left to be "washed," that is, the brick on the edge are again laid flat, and the rain falls upon them. Some clays will stand this, but the brick made of other clays are entirely destroyed, if not by rain, then by sun, as they break in half as the heat again strikes them. Brick that will stand "washing" are wheeled into the shed and set for salmon or arch bricks, when they go into kiln. The brick having been exposed to the rain are called "washed brick"; they have a rough appearance, and are generally not much esteemed, but they make the strongest brick that

comes out of the kiln; and when hard-burned, they have no equal for foundation or sewer work. (Davis 1885, 93)

The thirteen sample bricks at Timbuctoo fit this definition. Their color and texture have the characteristics of washer brick. However, their density and size did not adhere to standards for washer brick. The improper firing and low density of these thirteen sample bricks would have made them susceptible to the elements if they were used in foundation work. We wanted to understand how our sample bricks would stand up to the specifications of turn-of-the century trade manuals. We did some experimental archaeology to test the quality of the thirteen bricks using two contemporary instructional manuals for home building (Powell 1879; Churchill and Wickenden 1923).

Brick Testing

First, we measured the bricks and noted their coloring. George Powell (1879, 30) stated that $8\frac{3}{8}$ inches long, 4 inches wide, and $2\frac{3}{8}$ inches thick were the standard for brick manufactured in Trenton, New Jersey. The tested sample sizes range in length from $7\frac{3}{8}$ to $8\frac{9}{16}$ inches. The width ranged from $3\frac{3}{4}$ to $4\frac{5}{8}$ inches, and the thickness of the bricks ranged from $1\frac{7}{8}$ to $2\frac{1}{4}$ inches. As Table 5.1 shows, the measurements of the sample bricks vary considerably from the standard sizes Powell described for Trenton brick. The range in size and color of the Timbuctoo brick suggests they were handmade and were either fired in a scove kiln or in a wet clamp at Timbuctoo.

However, we wanted to understand the quality of the bricks according to late-nineteenth- and early twentieth-century building standards. To do so, we used Allen Churchill and Leonard Wickenden's *The House Owner's Book* (1923), an instruction manual for people interested in home construction. Churchill and Wickenden stated that "a good brick is one which will resist the disintegrating effects of weather—particularly, of frost. The first essential is that it should be well burned" (27). The authors offered the reader three tests. We used two of the three tests on a sample of six bricks to compare the quality of the Davis bricks. The third test required chemicals and acid that were beyond our means.

The first test we conducted involved striking the brick: "The simplest method of testing a brick is to strike it with a hammer. If it gives a clear, ringing sound, it is well burned. If the sound is deadened, or dull, the brick is soft-burned, or contains cracks" (Churchill and Wickenden 1923, 27). In our testing, only one of the six sample bricks, F130505c, had a distinctive ringing sound. Another brick, F130505b, which was partially vitrified, had a ringing sound when struck on the vitrified portion but a thud when it was hit in the middle. All of the other four bricks had a deadened, dull sound when they were hit. Two of the samples broke when they were lightly hit by the hammer. Only one of the bricks passed the first of Churchill and Wickenden's tests.

The second test quantifies the water absorption of the brick.

Dry the brick in the oven, weigh it carefully, then place it in boiling water for about five hours, leave it in the water until the latter has cooled, then remove the brick and weigh it again. The weight of the dry brick, subtracted from that of the wet brick, will give the weight of water absorbed. . . . For soft clay bricks, it should not exceed one-sixth. (Churchill and Wickenden 1923, 27)

Following these directions, we first placed the sample brick in an oven at a temperature of 200 degrees Fahrenheit for one hour. After allowing the bricks to cool, we weighed them. Next, we put the sample in a pot of boiling water for five hours. We then placed the brick in cool water for one hour. Finally, we removed the bricks, wiped off the excess water, and weighed them. Our results show that all of the brick samples except for F130505c (the sample that had passed the ring test) absorbed more than one-sixth of their dry weight.

These tests are subjective and are by no means scientific. However, the goal of our tests was to compare the bricks to the standards of turn-of-the-century building practices.

The results are given in table 5.1. From the total sample, only F130505c passed both the hammer and absorption tests. However, the measurements of that brick (which is 8 inches long, 3³/₁₆ inches wide, and 2¼ inches thick) are still outside the standards Powell gave for bricks produced in Trenton in the late 1870s (1879, 30). Powell advised brick workers to "reject all bad shaped and unsound brick. Good bricks are regular in shape, with plain surfaces and sharp, true angles" (28). What we see from our foray into experimental archaeology is that by all measures, the sample bricks (and by our observation most of the foundation bricks at the Davis site) would have failed to meet the building standards of the late nineteenth and early twentieth centuries. So why were they used in the foundation of the Davis house? The quality of the bricks suggests that they were part

Table 5.1. Summary of tests of bricks from the Davis Site

Brick #	Size	Color	Dry Weight	Wet Weight	Weight Difference	Less/Greater than ⅙ Dry Weight	Sound test	Fail/Pass	Comments
F130603a	7⅜" long, 3¾" wide, 1⅞" tall	Salmon	3 lb. 3 oz.	4 lb. 8 oz.	1 lb. 5 oz.	Greater	Ring	Fail	Poorly fired washer brick
F130603b	8⁹⁄₁₆" long, 4⅝" wide, 2¼" tall	Salmon	4 lb. 8 oz.	6 lb. 9 oz.	2 lb. 1 oz.	Greater	Dull	Fail	Broke when hit
F130505a	8⅛" long, 4³⁄₁₆" wide, 2" tall	Red	4 lb. 6 oz.	5 lb. 5 oz.	15 oz.	Greater	Dull	Fail	Poorly struck brick
F130505b	8¹⁄₁₆" long, 4¹⁄₁₆" wide, 2¹⁄₁₆" tall	Semi-vitrified	3 lb. 12 oz.	5 lb. 7 oz.	2 lb. 11 oz.	Greater	Ring and dull	Fail	Arch brick: ring on semi-vitrified portion, dull on red
F130505c	8" long, 3³⁄₁₆" wide, 2¼" tall	Cherry red	4 lb. 10 oz.	5 lb. 1 oz.	7 oz.	Less	Ring	Pass	Washer brick; pass, although smaller than standard brick
F130505d	8¼" long, 4¹⁄₁₆" wide, 2⅛" tall	Red	5 lb. 6 oz.	6 lb. 1 oz.	1 lb. 11 oz.	Greater	Dull	Fail	Broke when hit

of a tradition of making do. By the 1870s, brickmaking by hand in scove kilns and wet clamps had been almost completely replaced by machine manufacturing (Lynch 1994, 22). The sampled bricks were likely meant to be washer brick used specifically for underground work. However, as our testing showed, all of the sample bricks would likely have been rejected because of their size, density, and/or their water absorption. At the turn of the century, well-fashioned, machine-made bricks were expensive and out of reach for many impoverished people like the Davises. However, in a region that had no stone, slate, or other readily available natural resources for building structures, bricks, even those of inferior quality, were still the best materials for a foundation. While they were at risk of cracking over time (and many did), improperly fired, irregular, porous bricks were still better for building a foundation than wood. Acquiring inferior bricks at a reduced price that a brickyard had rejected and/or constructing an onsite wet clamp enabled William Davis to construct a home using the best resources he could obtain. Houses are more than shelter from the elements, they are our homes; the places where we live, love, and raise our families. Even though the poor quality bricks of the foundation did not meet the standards of the time drawing from a habitus of making do William ensured that his family would have a home.

6

FOOD, STRIFE, AND PRESERVATION

Because food is necessary for survival, all archaeologists focus on its production, preparation, consumption, and conservation. In this chapter, I discuss the influence of global events (World War I, the Great Depression, and World War II) and how race, class, and gender influenced everyday practices at Timbuctoo. I discuss two types of glassware artifacts: jars associated with home canning and jars associated with commercially processed food, especially peanut butter. These examples illustrate how people in Black households in Timbuctoo used commodity selection to survive in a context of economic marginalization. Commodified home canning paraphernalia and commercially processed foods were relatively new products in the late nineteenth century, and their presence at Timbuctoo illustrates the reflexive disposition of habitus. Timbuctoo residents canned their own food and purchased carefully selected processed foods because they understood the social and economic benefits of doing so. In periods marked by food scarcity, canning food at home and eating peanut butter were powerful tactics for keeping a family healthy.

Home Canning

The mass commodification of glass jars for home canning in the United States developed after the Civil War (Collins 1924, 238–239). The assemblage of home canning items from Timbuctoo dates from the late nineteenth to mid-twentieth centuries. However, the majority of artifacts date from 1910 to the 1940s. I want to focus on that time, when two world wars and a global economic depression occurred and affected the everyday lives of individuals. In the following sections I analyze home canning and commodified foods at Timbuctoo as localized practices and responses to global events and systemic marginalization.

It is often difficult to identify fragments of glassware used for canning because the sherds are sometimes colorless. Thus, our interpretations and discussion of home canning at Timbuctoo are based primarily on whole glass vessels and embossed fragments. Most glass canning jars were light aqua or colorless and had wide-mouthed openings. Their lids were made of zinc and milk glass. We used artifact comparisons between whole vessels and fragments to determine the form and function of the sherds. An interpreted total of 137 home canning fragments and whole vessels, including jars and lids, were recovered from the interior of the Davis foundation that had been used as a community trash pit. This represents 1.68 percent of the total glassware assemblage. The minimum number of vessels (MNV) of thirty-five home canning jars was calculated from the number of glass bases. This represents 3.3 percent of the MNV of the total glassware assemblage. The overall number of possible jars is relatively low when using this conservative methodology; the actual number of home canning jars is likely greater than the totals presented here. The vessels recovered dated from 1869 to 1956. The average date of the assemblage is 1912.5, while the median date is 1921. The terminus post quem date of 1869 is based on the patent date of Boyd's milk glass canning lid. The terminus ante quem is based on a milk glass lid with the patent date of 1956, but this item was likely an outlier for the assemblage because it was recovered above the midden in the plow zone.

The fragmentary nature of the glass sherds prevented us from getting a date range narrower than eighty-seven years. However, given that the assemblage has a median date of 1921, the 1912 median date for home canning is a good representation. All of the jar fragments show extensive use wear, indicating that reuse of glass jars was a common practice in food canning, and the use life of jars and lids usually extended well past their manufacturing date.

We found very few tin can fragments (n = 122, MNV = 6). This low total is likely because the acidic soils corroded the thin metal. Additionally, home canning with tin cans in the twentieth century required expensive equipment and considerable skill (Hughes 1918). The absence of tin can fragments could also reflect wartime rationing, as metals were among the first resources the government commissioned for military use. On July 21, 1917, Congress passed the Lever Food Control Act, which said that the federal government had power over the supply and distribution of foods, fuel,

Figure 6.1. A World War I propaganda poster used to promote home canning for the war effort. The image was created by J. Paul Verrees for the 1918 National War Garden Commission. Source: Library of Congress Prints and Photographs Division, https://www.loc.gov/item/2003652822.

fertilizer, and feed in order to ensure national security. The government also had control over the ingredients, tools, and equipment needed to make such products (Dickson 1944, 20–21). As part of this responsibility, the government called on home canners to use glass jars rather than metal cans (see figure 6.1).

While the US military fought overseas during World War I, at home there was a war of conservation that affected consumer behavior and practices.

The government promoted conservation through wartime propaganda. Literature, rallies, and posters were strategies to discipline individuals into practicing conservation (see figure 6.1, and figure 6.2 for an example from World War II). Central to this propaganda was the concept that Americans had a collective identity, that all individual practices had direct effects on the US military (Bentley 1998).

Patriotic imagery emphasized that individuals belonged to a collective American community. For example, the *Progressive Farmer* stated that "there is only one way to win the war, [and it] is for us to be more efficient than the enemy" (1918, quoted in Dickson 1944, 41). Conserving food by canning at home was an important part of this discourse of wartime discipline. The United States Food Administration, a new government agency that was created in 1917 to promote food conservation, produced posters with slogans such as "Food Saving was at first a fad; then a patriotic service; now a habit," and "U-Boats and wastefulness are twin enemies" (United States Food Administration, quoted in Dickson 1944, 43).

Government efforts to promote food conservation were often directed toward women. For example, in May 1917, the State Foods Council and the Women's National Defense Council urged women to "Serve by Saving" in order to promote household conservation (Dickson 1944, 60). However, the government encouraged citizens to limit the consumption of sugar and, to a lesser extent, salt. These two ingredients are heavily used in food preservation. To encourage people to comply with the voluntary conservation measures, the government created the National War Garden Commission to educate people about new ways of conserving food. American housewives were to use the recent innovation of cold packing to conserve food and limit items such as sugar (National Magazine 1917).

Cold packing fruits and vegetables entailed several steps. First, vegetables or fruits were washed. Then the produce was blanched in boiling water for three to five minutes. It was then quickly placed into cold water, next removed, drained, and packed into sterilized glass jars as tightly as possible. Finally, the jars were filled with hot water and sealed (National Magazine 1918, 4–5). The government used propaganda such as pamphlets, posters, and public lectures to advertise the benefits of home canning through cold packing:

> Home canning is the most effective of all methods of conserving food products. It is a time-honored custom that has been gradually

eliminated in most American homes. It was formerly an arduous and expensive task. Today science has made it inexpensive and easy, with the chance of spoilage practically eliminated. This revolution in home canning has come through the adoption of what is known as the cold-pack method. (National Magazine 1918, 3)

In addition to distributing literature, schools and social organizations formed canning clubs to transform a largely individual practice into a community one that called for home canners to conserve foods that the US military needed (Collins 1924, 240):

Every woman can render important services to the nation in its present emergency. She need not leave her home or abandon her home duties to help the armed forces. She can help to feed and clothe our armies and help to supply food to those beyond the seas by practicing effective thrift in her own household. Every ounce of food the housewife saves from being wasted in her home—all the food which she or her children produce in the garden and can or preserve—every garment which care and skillful repair make it unnecessary to replace—all lessen that household's draft on the already insufficient world supplies. (National Magazine 1917, 15)

The government made specific efforts to recruit Black people into wartime food conservation. Herbert Hoover, the head of the Food Administration, addressed the need for Black people to participate in food conservation on April 12, 1918:

Our Nation is engaged in a war for its very existence. To win this war we must save food, grow great crops of foodstuffs and substitute other foods for those most easily shipped to our associate in this war and our own soldiers in France, thousands of whom are men of your own race. The Food Administration realizes that the Negro people of this Nation can be of the utmost help in food conservation and food production. Every Negro man, woman and child can render a definite service by responding to the appeal and instructions of the Food Administration and its representatives. The Negroes have shown themselves loyal and responsive in every national crisis. Their greatest opportunity of the present day, to exercise this loyalty, is to help save and grow food. I am confident that they will respond to the suggestions of the Food Administration and thus prove again their patriotism for the winning of this war. (quoted in Dickson 1944, 75)

The government recruited Black churches, social organizations, and businesses to promote the conservation of food and even created a Negro Press Section to create informational short films for movie theaters and literature for Black newspapers and schools (Dickson 1944, 73). Even W. E. B. Du Bois became part of the discourse on Black wartime rationing practices; he stated in 1918 that "here now in the stress of war comes a chance to correct bad habits. . . . Food conservation is not all evil; rather it spells opportunity for the learning of better food habits" (quoted in Dickson 1944, 75). While Du Bois was commenting specifically on the dietary practices of white and Black Americans that included consuming too much sugar, his statement was an appeal for food conservation (Dickson 1944, 75–76). These disciplining practices of food conservation served the US military well and helped it contribute to the Allied victory.

Following the war, the United States enjoyed a brief era of economic prosperity. Bentley (1998, 131) argues that because of this prosperity, the need for home canning diminished as American housewives switched to purchasing commercially canned food. However, as the nation slipped into the Great Depression, the need for frugal home economics caused a rebirth of household canning. During the Depression of 1929–1940, unemployment in the United States hovered around 17 percent (Mullins et al. 2011). The economic realities of mass impoverishment meant that individual households had to come together to survive. This communalism and collective identity contrasted with the ideology of individualism that typified the 1920s (Bentley 1998). Many Black people did not experience the broad trends in the history of this period, including the collective identity the government promoted during World War I and the individualistic ideologies of the 1920s because their experience of racialized marginalization had led them to cultivate their own unique, yet heterogeneous, collective ideology. From the period of enslavement through the era of Jim Crow, Black communities used collectivism as a strategy for contesting and circumnavigating repression. While there were (and are) distinct regional, temporal, and social differences within Black America, everyday experiences of structural racism transcend such differences to create a collective identity among many Black communities.

Food conservation was part of this learned practice of perseverance because it often meant survival (Palmer 2011, 151). The rural setting of

Figure 6.2. A World War II propaganda poster used to promote home canning for the war effort. Ration points were used during the war to limit the consumption of goods. The image was created by Dick Williams for the War Food Administration in 1944. Source: USDA National Agricultural Library Special Collections Exhibits, https://www.nal.usda. gov/exhibits/speccoll/items/show/245.

Timbuctoo was conducive to food conservation practices; home canning meant that summer gardens resulted in winter meals. In contrast to urban settings, where during the Great Depression most families had to consume what food they could when they could get it instead of preserving food for the future (Hunter 1989), people in rural areas could preserve summer surpluses for the winter. The oral histories offered by the village elders are replete with stories of them as children working on nearby farms and enjoying harvests of apples, corn, plums, peaches, and tomatoes.

The home canning efforts during the period 1917–1945 are seen as being quite successful in America. Bentley (1998, 132) comments that in many rural areas impoverished women practiced subsistence gardening and canning as a necessary tactic for family survival. The temporal range of the food canning assemblage at the Davis Site and the relevant historical records underscore the lower economic status of many of the residents. The home canning practices in Timbuctoo fit this discourse of necessity. Although the oral histories of elders from Timbuctoo do not discuss home canning, they mention picking foods such as tomatoes and peaches in childhood. Given the archaeological evidence of home canning, some of these fruits and vegetables may have been preserved by the elders' families. For impoverished people, food preservation could mean the difference between empty and full bellies in the leaner months.

Commercial Canned Foods

In this section I discuss the consumption of commercial canned food as a tactic impoverished people use to provide sustenance while also saving them time and energy. This discussion of commodified foods fits into Bourdieu's (1984, 200) discussion of how the dietary practices of the working classes are often characterized in functional terms. He argues that for the working classes, meals center on foods that are high in fat, calories, carbohydrates, and protein and are often inexpensive (190). This may seem obvious to us, but it is important to understand the economic realities that impoverished people face, their access to foods, and the nutritional needs that many have because of the type of work they do. These practices of food consumption are influenced by the energy needs associated with manual labor that calls for high-calorie foods:

> Thus it is possible to deduce the popular tastes for the foods that are simultaneously most "filling" and the most economical from the necessity of reproducing labor power at the lowest cost which is forced on the proletariat as its very definition. The idea of taste, typically bourgeois, since it presupposes absolute freedom of choice, is so closely associated with the idea of freedom that many people find it hard to grasp the paradoxes of the taste of necessity. (177–178)

Bourdieu argues that in contrast, food for the bourgeoisie is a disciplined art form, a medium for displaying the individual's refinement. He asserts that the bourgeoisie do not consume food solely for sustenance as the working classes do.

Another factor that influences food consumption is an individual's socialization into preexisting structures of taste. We may feel that taste is subjective for the individual, but a person's tastes are created and sustained by what they have access to, which can be influenced by variables such as culture, access to economic resources, geographical region, religion, and social structures. Bourdieu wrote that

> some simply sweep [taste] aside, making practice a direct product of economic necessity, failing to realize that necessity can only be fulfilled, most of the time, because the agents are inclined to fulfill it, because they have a taste for what they are anyway condemned to. (Bourdieu 1984, 178)

Bourdieu provides the example of a foreman who makes more money than a clerical white-collar worker yet still prefers the inexpensive and high-calorie foods of the working classes. Although he could afford the more expensive, artful dishes that symbolize his economic status, his individual tastes are the result of how he was socialized (1984, 177). Bourdieu posited that the structures and practices of everyday life resulted in a cycle in which the structure, habitus, and practice are not mutually exclusive but influence one another. Thus, the foreman's socialization into preexisting structures influences his diet (200).

Commercially canned food developed as a mass-produced commodity after the Civil War (Collins 1924, 238–239). Commercial canning grew because of several interrelated factors. First, processed foods were advertised as healthy options for middle-class households (Hunter 1989). Moreover, canned foods were examples of conspicuous consumption that could advertise the social and economic identity of the household. Families in the Midwest could dine on canned oysters, people in the Northeast could enjoy peaches in the winter months, and Californians could consume Atlantic cod (Bitting and Bitting 1916).

Second, in the latter half of the nineteenth century, advances in machine canning and increased competition among canneries decreased prices, enabling the working classes to purchase the products of the growing canned food industry (Neil 1914; Bitting and Bitting 1916; Collins 1924). In *Canning and How to Use Canned Foods,* Bitting and Bitting (1916) argued that commercially canned foods were more economical than fresh food.

> The relative cost of canned and fresh stock is not well understood. Any estimate made to determine which is the cheaper should include not only the first cost of raw material, but also the added labor in securing the material, in its preparation, and in the disposal of the waste. (91)

As the prices of commodified foods decreased, impoverished people had greater access to foods that could help them save on time and energy. While the initial cost of canned food may have kept some consumers away, manufacturers and advertisers argued that when the monetary cost was compared to the costs of time, resources, and energy used in homemade foods, commercially produced foods were more economical. "Wise economy demands that the feeding-stuffs which are at command shall be so combined that there shall be no waste of either material or energy" (Condit and Long 1914, 6). The turn of the twentieth century marked the transition of the household from a site of production to a site of consumption. Women were central in this social and economic shift:

> Time was when the woman who kept house was expected to be the high priestess of that dire goddess How-to-Save-Money, but her metamorphosis from producer to consumer has shifted her worship to the new deity How-to-Spend. From an all-round producer the American woman had become the greatest consumer in the world. (Bruère and Bruère 1912, 181)

After the Civil War, 53 percent of the United States population was engaged in farming (Cross 2000, 18). In the late nineteenth and early twentieth centuries, many household farms became focused on large-scale cash crops (Cross 2000, 2). Self-sustaining farm households became a thing of the past as the processed food market demanded an ever-increasing supply of produce and livestock. The development of commercially canned food offered both rural and urban households an inexpensive, easily accessible, and diverse array of foods that were not restricted by season or geography.

However, the economic value of canned foods was not measured simply by price (Bitting and Bitting 1916, 91). Time and energy savings were another important benefit of canned foods. Commercially prepared condiments were seen as time savers that could also enhance household meals. Condit and Long (1914, 192) urged consumers that with the use of spices and condiments, "the cheaper and less attractive staple of foods can be given distinction and flavor, and the cook will acquire a reputation for skill and judgment."

The commercial canning industry and its products were not simply a reflection of changes in society; they were also constitutive of those changes in the first half of the twentieth century. The popularity of consuming processed foods fostered the development of a consumer habitus that sought to balance the dietary needs and expenditures of the household within the ever-expanding marketplace. This balancing act created, modified, and reproduced a socialized practice of selecting what and what not to purchase.

Economically marginalized consumers of Timbuctoo in the twentieth century did not always purchase the least expensive items and they did not always make their own food in order to save money. They weighed a variety of factors that included taste, time, energy, money, and other resources as they decided when to process food at home and when to purchase commercially processed food. A new habitus of a well-educated and savvy consumer was the result of expanding diversity in the price, availability, and product of processed foods (Mullins 2011). Consumption was no longer just an individual practice but was transformed into a science that sought to increase home efficiency (Bruère and Bruère 1912, 181).

This brings us to a discussion of one particular type of commodified food found at Timbuctoo: peanut butter.

Peanut Butter Jars at Timbuctoo

Identifying the specific product that was contained in a bottle, can, or jar can be difficult. While the majority of commercially produced foods were packaged in metal cans, these products are underrepresented in the archaeological record at Timbuctoo. Many companies embossed mold numbers or product codes on the base of the glassware they used, but most glassware did not provide information about what it contained. However, some companies worked directly with manufacturers of glass bottles to create distinctive container forms and/or embossing that identified their brand or specific products. We can use the documentary record (advertisements, trade catalogs, and photos) to provide possible interpretations of what may have been in the food containers.

Three complete glass jars have the words "Peanut Butter" embossed on their base and two jars (one complete and one partial vessel) have images of peanuts embossed on their walls in the Timbuctoo assemblage. While the

Figure 6.3. A peanut butter jar made by Hazel-Atlas (1937–1964) that was recovered from Davis site trash midden. Photo by Christopher P. Barton.

five glass jars represent less than 0.0003 percent of the total assemblage, the embossed labeling represents a rare identification of the contents of commercial food jars at Timbuctoo. The percentage of peanut butter jars that were originally tossed into the midden is likely much larger than the five-vessel sample, but we will never know what that percentage was because of the deterioration of paper labeling and manufacturers' use of general form jars for a diverse range of products.

Figure 6.3 is a glass jar with embossed peanuts on its walls. The front wall of the jar has an undecorated circle for the paper label. Based on associated artifacts, the jar dates to the period 1937–1948. A review of contemporary trade catalogs and advertisements suggests that this peanut butter jar was likely not made by or for a national brand and may have been made for a regional or local grocery store.

The base of a four-sided peanut butter jar is embossed with the words "ASCO" followed by "PEANUT BUTTER" under the brand name and the maker's mark for the Capstan Glass Company. The company, which was located in Connellsville, Pennsylvania, was in operation from 1919 to 1938 and often made bottles and jars to meet specific requests of their customers. Three peanut butter jars from Timbuctoo are from such a special order. The word "ASCO" is an acronym for American Stores Company, a chain of grocery stores that was formed when several Philadelphia grocery stores merged in 1917 (Mayo 1993, 84–85).

National brands of peanut butter did not appear until the 1920s (Krampner 2013). In the early twentieth century, most peanut butter was purchased from local stores. Stores would have tubs of peanut butter that would be ladled into tin cans or glass jars (Krampner 2013, 26).

Food historian Jon Krampner (2013, 20–23) argues that the peanut has a pejorative legacy in the United States because of its association with the diets of economically marginalized groups and its use as livestock feed. During the period of slavery, southern planters gave enslaved people peanuts to eat because of their high yield and low cost. The racially charged term "peanut gallery" comes from the segregation era; it refers to a separate area, often a balcony, in many theaters that was farthest away from the stage where Black patrons could sit (Weyeneth 2005, 19). The connections between peanuts and class resulted in peanuts being associated with the poor. As a result of its low economic return for farmers, peanuts were not extensively grown before the twentieth century (Smith 2002; Krampner 2013). Despite popular belief, the famed scientist George Washington Carver did not invent peanut butter. Historians are unable to credit a single person with inventing peanut butter, as several people claimed to have invented it by the turn of the twentieth century (Krampner 2013, 26).

It is possible that John Harvey Kellogg invented peanut butter. Kellogg, a Seventh-day Adventist and physician, operated the Western Health Reform Institute in Battle Creek, Michigan. One of the tenets of Seventh-day Adventist Church is the belief that God made humans the stewards of the earth. Seventh-day Adventists believe in healthy living, and many are vegetarians (Krampner 2013, 28). In the early 1890s, Kellogg developed a meat substitute made from peanuts for his patients who suffered from digestive and dental problems. Instead of roasting the nuts, Kellogg boiled them for several hours, then ground them into a paste with a bit of salt. Kellogg stated that his peanut product was "the most delicious nut butter that you have ever tasted in your life" and that it was "perfectly digestible" (quoted in Smith 2002, 32). In 1895, Kellogg filed a patent application for a product that was "moist, pasty, adhesive and brown, which for distinction is termed 'butter' or 'paste'" (quoted in Smith 2002, 32–33). In 1897, Sanitas, a Kellogg company, advertised "Nut Butters" in trade and grocery catalogs, but because they used steamed rather than roasted peanuts, they were quite bitter and were not very popular with consumers (Krampner 2013, 29–30). In addition, the farm acreage devoted to growing peanuts was small in the 1890s, which limited the supply of peanut butter. As a result, it was primarily used as a health food for patients. However, the nature of supply and demand meant that peanut butter became a relatively expensive, high-end food. The middle and upper classes ate salads, meals, and soups made with peanut butter in posh tearooms and fine restaurants at the turn of the twentieth century (Smith 2002, 30; Krampner 2013, 26). The bitter nut spread was often mixed with a variety of other ingredients, including mayonnaise, heavy cream, lemon juice, applesauce, mustard, and catsup (Peanut Promoter 1922, 12).

Peanut cultivation changed because of environmental and social events. In 1903, the boll weevil (*Anthonomus grandis*) decimated the cotton industry in the South (Krampner 2013, 38–39). In an attempt to assist southern planters, the United States Department of Agriculture urged them to grow more diverse crops, including the peanut. The following year, peanut butter was exhibited at the World's Fair in St. Louis, Missouri. By the 1910s, the popularity of peanuts had assisted in the recovery of the southern farming economy, resulting in an increased supply of peanuts that led to a drop in the price of peanut butter (Smith 2002, 87; Krampner 2013, 47). Within ten years from the time peanut butter was invented, it began to be a common staple in the American diet. In the early twentieth century, "It was a delicacy in tea rooms in New York and Boston until the price dropped. When that happened and anyone could buy it, it went out of the upper class and into the lower class" (Krampner 2013, 26).

As it became part of the everyday working-class diet, manufacturers began to emphasize how nutritious and inexpensive peanut butter was and to produce advertisements that informed consumers that it was a good substitute for meat. This information filtered into the home economics texts, home canning manuals, and news articles:

A peanut butter sandwich is quite as nourishing as a meat sandwich. (Cocroft 1912, 165)

Let me tell you that peanut butter is the most highly nutritious food we have because it contains one and one-half times as much protein, over three times as much fat, and over three times as much fuel value as round steak. In addition, it contains 17 per cent of carbohydrates, totally lacking in steak. (quoted in Bitting and Bitting 1916, 102)

Peanut butter, according to specialists of the United States Department of Agriculture, contains 16 times as much protein, over three times as much fat, and three times as much fuel value as round steak. Also, about 17 percent of peanut butter is carbohydrates, mostly starch, while steak contains no carbohydrates. These figures show that, pound for pound, peanut butter has a much greater food value than round steak.[1]

While the popularity of peanut butter grew throughout the 1910s, food rationing during World War I was the main reason that peanut butter became a quintessential American food. During the war, the United States Food Administration urged Americans to consume peanuts and peanut products instead of wheat and meat, two products the government needed to feed the US military (Krampner 2013, 44). The Beech-Nut company, a peanut butter manufacturer, claimed that peanut butter was a "new patriotic way to conserve animals" (quoted in Krampner 2013, 45). During the war, the unshelled nuts took up too much space during transportation, so manufacturers switched to processed peanut products, especially, peanut butter (Smith 2002, 89).

The campaigns to increase peanut butter consumption succeeded. The production of peanut butter increased from 1899, when 2 million pounds were produced, to 1919, when 158 million pounds of peanut butter were produced (Krampner 2013, 44–45).

During the Great Depression, peanut butter offered impoverished people an inexpensive food that was high in fat, protein, and calories (Smith 2002; Krampner 2013, 72). When commercially produced pre-sliced bread became available in 1928, a layer of peanut butter combined with tomatoes, lettuce, jelly, jam, and/or preserves provided people with a fast, inexpensive, yet nutritionally complete meal.

The nutritional qualities of peanut butter were again underscored as food rationing restricted civilian meat consumption during World War II. In an effort to conserve meat supplies for military use, the government initiated "Meatless Day" programs. The USDA provided pamphlets containing meatless recipes that emphasized the protein content of nuts and beans. During the war the military issued C-rations (field rations) and K-rations (survival rations) that contained peanut butter to provide calories in a small portable package for front-line soldiers (Krampner 2013, 80).

For economically marginalized people, like many of the residents of Timbuctoo, peanut butter offered an inexpensive and nutritious source of protein that was less expensive than meat purchased from the butcher or from their own slaughtered livestock. Like other commodified foods, peanut butter saved time and energy. For people living in poverty, time, energy, and money were valuable resources that needed to be practically rationed. The inclusion of peanut butter and commodified food into individual practice underscores the reflexive disposition of habitus of negotiating poverty.

Racist practices worked to ensure that Black people stayed in the lowest economic positions in American society. Limited economic capital and systemic obstacles to political, social, and educational opportunities forced many Black people to improvise in order to survive. During World War I, the Great Depression, and World War II, most Americans were introduced to a habitus of saving and practicing food conservation. However, for many Black people, conserving food was a continuation of practices that dated back many decades; it was part of the survival strategies they used as marginalized people (Orser 1998, 2004; Palmer 2011; Wilkie 2000; Mullins et al. 2011). From the period of enslavement through the era of Jim Crow, Black people had to develop unique survival tactics to resist repression (Orser 1998, 2004; Mullins 1999a; Wilkie 2000; Mullins et al. 2011).

The consumption of peanut butter fits within Bourdieu's discourse of taste. While peanut butter consumption at Timbuctoo was influenced by individual taste, that taste was structured by social conventions and practices. Peanut butter offered impoverished peoples during the turbulent periods of World War I, the Great Depression, and World War II an inexpensive and highly nutritious staple to their diet. For many of the Timbuctoo residents, who balanced considerations of time, energy, and money with their need for protein, fat, and calories, peanut butter was an excellent food choice. The presence of peanut butter in people's diets at Timbuctoo underscores the reflexive disposition of social practice, taste, and habitus. In the period 1919–1948, the estimated date range for the peanut butter assemblage at Timbuctoo, the mass commodification of peanut butter was less than fifteen years old, yet residents incorporated it into their diet because of its functionality, underscoring Bourdieu's thesis (1984, 200) that for impoverished peoples, the primary purpose of food is to nourish the body.

7

DISPLAY AND DESIRE

The underlying focus of this book has been how race and class affected the lives of Timbuctoo residents. I have argued that people operate within a habitus created through strife and perseverance. Material culture played important roles in constructing that habitus: it reflected and reproduced social structures, ideologies, and practices. Objects are important to people because they reflect the values of society, and through people's use of objects we reproduce those same values.

This chapter complicates the narrative of poverty by discussing how people use objects to contest being labeled as socially inferior. Consumer culture is not always based on rational decisions made by powerless consumers. While people living in poverty have limited access to the marketplace, they can still be empowered by the decisions they make. In this chapter, I situate a sample of the bric-a-brac artifacts from Timbuctoo within the social and historical contexts of consumerism in a capitalist society. During the period 1890–1940, the ideology of individualism and the advertising of mass-produced commodities changed the relationships between people and objects (Schlereth 1981; Mullins 1999a, 1999b, 2011; Matt 2003, 182–184). I also discuss this bric-a-brac sample within the context of a discourse of the relationship between identity construction and material culture. While the archaeological record of Timbuctoo illustrates how an impoverished community used material culture to contest their marginalization, it also illustrates how individuals used objects with symbolic meaning to satisfy their aspirations and desires.

To better understand how we arrived at these interpretations at Timbuctoo, we must contextualize some of the broader trends in theoretical historical archaeology dealing with consumerism. Some archaeologists who study consumption practices remove all agency from working-class individuals. These models draw on Thorstein Veblen's *A Theory of the Leisure Class* (1899). Veblen theorized that middle- and working-class people emulate the practices of the upper class as a way to construct genteel identities. In his study of the enslaved people's quarters at Kingsmill Plantation in Williamsburg, Virginia, William Kelso (1984) did not believe that any of the artifacts he uncovered were related to African practices and concluded that enslaved people only imitated white culture. Kelso wrote, "Of course, winning favor of the master must have been great incentive for the blacks to mimic the white culture and to suppress quickly any very visible African tradition" (201). Assimilationist interpretations such as this one reduce the choices of marginalized people to practices of imitation, eliminating individual agency people exercise as they construct their identities (Mullins 2011, 116–117).

Many of the early studies of the everyday lives of both enslaved and free Black people centered on their socioeconomic status, a term that incorrectly conflates social and economic identities, practices, and beliefs (Cook et al. 1996, 51). Social identity and economic status are two different concepts. For example, a professor may have limited economic capital, but she has increased social status in society because of her social capital as an expert. The term socioeconomic is problematic because it further excludes factors such as region, race, ethnicity, class, and religion that could affect the practices of consumers (Cook et al. 1996, 52; Mullins 2011, 20). This usage drew on a model that was guided by the concept of consumer choice, which sought to situate the archaeological record within quantitative patterning and empiricism as a way of understanding socioeconomic status (Cook et al. 1996, 51–52; Mullins 2011, 22).[1]

An example of such work is the price index George Miller (1980) constructed for nineteenth-century white-bodied English ceramics. Miller's research uncovered price-fixing agreements between English manufacturers of ceramics, both undecorated cream-colored wares and highly decorated, transfer-printed, and hand-painted tablewares. The index he constructed provided archaeologists with a method for determining the relative cost of ceramic assemblages. While the index is a useful tool, archaeologists often used it as a proxy for socioeconomic status. Using a consumer choice framework and a price index without looking at other factors ignores the historical and ethnographical evidence that help researchers understand the socioeconomic status of a household (Cook et al. 1996, 52–53).

In contrast, Lauren Cook, Rebecca Yamin, and John McCarthy (1996) argue that the consumer choice model does not address *why* individuals make choices as consumers. Instead, it restricts complex archaeological data to reductionist patterns by overemphasizing the monetary and utilitarian value of objects. They argue that we need to understand that individual consumers are "conscious and knowing users and shapers of culture" (Cook et al. 1996, 50–51). Individuals exercise considerable agency when they make decisions about what to buy. Consumption thus becomes a core component of how individuals and communities construct identities (50–53, 57). Archaeologists who subscribe to the consumer agency approach contextualize data using historical documents and oral histories in the hope that they will be able to learn the specific meanings behind the consumer decisions individuals made.

LouAnn Wurst and Randall McGuire (1999) argue that while understanding the meaning of the things consumers buy is important, Cook, Yamin, and McCarthy's approach overemphasizes the individual consumer at the expense of reaching an understanding of broader social networks. They argue that an individualistic approach to consumption universalizes the modern ideologies of autonomous individualism and consumer choice (193–196). Archaeologists who focus on an individual's agency in making purchasing decisions fail to put consumers who are on the social and economic peripheries of society into proper context. Wurst and McGuire argue that consumer choice is shaped by race, ethnicity, gender, religion, region, culture, and access to the marketplace. All of these can either increase or limit the choices a consumer has. This is important to understand when discussing the everyday lives of people, like those at Timbuctoo, who lived in a society shaped by racism and classism that limited their opportunities.

Wurst and McGuire (1999, 196–197) argue that in the nineteenth century, advertisers promoted the idea that consumption was a vehicle for upward social mobility. But many members of the working class did not have the economic resources to fully participate in the new consumer culture; they were able to be consumers only in order to meet their basic needs. Wurst and McGuire contend that the developing consumer revolution was a mixed blessing for the working classes of the United States. On one hand, people who once could not participate joined the ever-expanding consumer culture to purchase goods and exercise some power in consumer markets. On the other hand, this involvement removed any hope of class consciousness and replaced it with the illusion of equality through consumption

(Wurst and McGuire 1999, 197). In Wurst and McGuire's view, working-class consumers participate in their own repression. In the late nineteenth century, consumers demanded low prices, manufacturers cut labor costs, which hurt working-class people, a vicious pattern that continues today. However, Wurst and McGuire maintain that people still have some power when they make choices as consumers.

These theoretical models in historical archaeology—the consumer choice model that emphasizes the power of the individual consumer and the Marxist analysis that largely sees consumers as passive victims of a structure that represses them—leave us in a precarious position where each theory is on opposite ends of a spectrum that explains consumer behavior.

To address these concerns, we turn to the work of Paul Mullins (1999a, 1999b, 2001, 2011) who incorporates elements of the Marxist-structural approach with elements of the emphasis on the individual that is the hallmark of consumer studies. Mullins defines consumption as

> a complex and far-reaching concept that in various scholars' hands encompasses the gamut of making, selling, buying, using, and discarding material things. At its heart consumption revolves around the acquisition of things to confirm, display, accent, mask, and imagine who we are and whom we wish to be. Material consumption may instrumentally display social status, evoke ethnicity or exhibit gender, but it also can be an unexpressed process of self-definition and collective identification. (Mullins 2011, 2)

This definition expands the traditional framework of consumption beyond the acquisition of commodities into an approach that includes the reflexive and constitutive roles material culture plays in social life. Mullins argues that archaeologists should understand that consumption is a multifaceted practice that includes everything people do with the material objects they acquire.

Mullins (2011, 39) points out that people do not always buy things to emphasize their individual middle-class status through public display; instead, individuals often use the objects they buy for their own private purposes. This approach challenges the perspective that individuals consume objects so they can imitate the upper classes. Mullins recasts consumption as a self-oriented practice of individual desire. He defines desires as

> socially conditioned, contextually distinctive, and idealistic aspirations played out in all material consumption. . . . Consumer desire

is not simply a never-ending cycle of the articulation of wants that are then satisfied with objects; it also cannot be reduced to conscious idealization that inevitably leads to disillusion because those ideals cannot be realized. Instead, desire articulates social contradictions in a way that mediates, attempts to reconcile, or appears to resolve incongruities. (Mullins 1999a, 31)

This is especially important for Black Americans, because they used their participation in consumerism to contest society's negative labeling of Black people as inferior. They also used consumerism to construct their own individual desires to belong to the middle class (Mullins 1999a, 32). It is not that the consumption of objects masked the very real social problems of society; rather, many Black Americans believed that the status they desired could be influenced through consumerism. Mullins argues that buying things did not create an illusion that masked very real social problems; rather, many Black people believed that the middle-class identity they desired could be achieved through consumerism (Mullins 1999a, 31–32). Mullins's approach does not ignore the structural influences that affect consumption (as the consumer choice model does). However, as he argues, the fact that these structures exist does not mean that individual desire and agency are meaningless (as Marxist theories claim). Instead, it is important to address the contexts that enable and/or limit an individual's ability to participate in consumer culture. While consumption can facilitate the reproduction of repression, as Wurst and McGuire argue, it can also be used to exercise individual agency and create specific meaning. Consumerism is shaped by both the subjectiveness of the individual and the structural influence of society (Mullins 2011, 144).

Capitalism is not just an economic system; it is a far-reaching complex network that influences nearly every aspect of life, including the cultural, economic, political, and social structures of society (Leone 2005; McGuire 2008; Matthews 2012). Its effects are so pervasive that they literally change how people see themselves and others. They turn social constructions into social structures and make ideologies seem like the natural state of existence (Pezzarossi 2019, 456).

In 1865, millions of formerly enslaved Black people entered a capitalist society. Operating from a fear that their presence threatened white hegemony, white people created new forms of racism to undermine Black social and political power. These fears manifested in new ideologies and pseudoscience that championed the biological, cultural, economic, political, and social superiority of the white race. The second half of the nineteenth century was when scientific racism flourished, southern whites prevented Black men from voting, white employers refused to hire Black workers, and racist depictions of Black people appeared in every aspect of popular culture. Racism permeated nearly every facet of US society (Roediger 1991; Orser 2007).

The expansion of structures of race developed sociopolitical movements in America, including the growth of consumer culture (Mullins 1999a, 166). Mass production, marketing, consumption, and the use of commodities changed the relationships between people and things. While capitalism destabilized the working classes, contaminated the environment, and fanned the flames of racial tensions, it gave marginalized peoples greater access to the consumer market (Leone 2005, 175; Smith 2007).

For the people at Timbuctoo, access to the marketplace offered a medium for constructing and displaying their desires related to middle class identity. The growth of consumer culture was accompanied by an ideology that stated that individual aspirations could be achieved, at least in part, through consumption. Black people, including the residents of Timbuctoo, used consumerism to construct and underscore their membership in the American middle class. They used the consumption and display of prosaic objects such as bric-a-brac to construct and reinforce their identity.

Bric-a-brac consists of a vast spectrum of mass-produced decorative and ornamental objects, including vases, figurines, statuary, lithographs, and tableware, that have been used in households since the mid-nineteenth century. One such example of these display wares from Timbuctoo is Depression glass, a term used to describe the glassware produced from the 1920s through the 1940s. The glass is of low to medium quality and comes in different colors, including green, cobalt blue, ruby red, amber, and amethyst; some has no color. The geometric and floral landscapes and themed designs on Depression glass reflect broader trends in popular culture following the Great Depression. These designs also appeared on ceramics, stationery, bric-a-brac, architecture, and other fashionable items (Schroy 2006, 7–8). Depression glass, like other forms of inexpensive bric-a-brac, was designed to look like more expensive objects, such as cut glass. The low quality of Depression glass is visible in the jagged edges, inconsistent patterns, and frequency of bubbles in the product. Despite its quality, Depression glass was a very popular product in the 1920s–1940s.

Depression glass items were sold for only a few pennies and could be purchased through mail-order catalogs and at local stores (Nutting 2003,

Figure 7.1. A Depression glass tumbler similar to one recovered at Timbuctoo, titled Florentine #1 that was made by Hazel-Atlas (1932–1935). Photo by Martin Chaffee.

447). It was produced in such mass quantities that cinemas, stores, and other businesses used it as giveaways during promotional events (Wilkie and Farnsworth 2011, 66). Some items of Depression glass were functional (e.g., bowls, glasses, plates), and some were intended for display (decorative pieces). Because of their colors and popular styles, impoverished people often used items made of Depression glass as display objects (Belk 1988, 160).

The Depression glass recovered from our excavations of the community trash midden was produced by the Hazel-Atlas Company, the Hocking Glass Company, and the Jeannette Glass Company. The recovered artifacts show no visible signs of use wear, such as scratches made by utensils, suggesting that the objects were curated by the owner. One tumbler made by the Hazel-Atlas Company in the period 1932–1935 is the Florentine #1 style (see figure 7.1). It measures 6 inches tall and 4 inches in diameter. The vessel is far too small for a serving vessel and the lack of use wear suggests that the object was used for decoration.

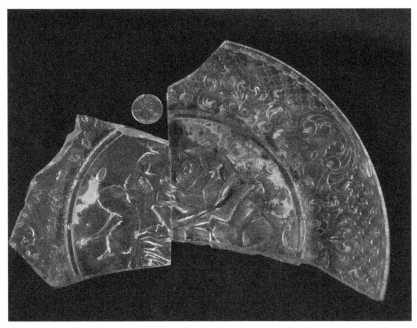

Figure 7.2. A pressed glass plate with floral motif (1920–1940) recovered from Davis site trash midden. Photo by Christopher P. Barton.

Similarly, a pressed glass plate was likely an inexpensive or promotional product. The plate was designed to look like more expensive cut glass (see figure 7.2). The motif is a floral design with a red painted rose in the center and green-colored vines and leaves on the exterior rim. The plate is of poor quality; it has visible mold imperfections and sharp, jagged edges on its design lines. The plate has no signs of use wear, suggesting that its owner curated and used it for display.

Finally, a candlestick holder from the assemblage, part of a two-piece set, is carnival glass. Popular from the 1920s–1940s, carnival glass is characterized by a mix of bright iridescent colors and stylish designs. Similar to Depression glass, carnival glassware was produced in a variety of forms and was so inexpensive that it was often given away as a prize at fairs where customers would throw pennies on carnival glass bowls, plates, and vases (Schroy 2006, 6). It is unknown how this candlestick holder was acquired, but like the tumbler and the plate, it was a decorative display piece.

Using bric-a-brac to signal identity challenged the racial and class hierarchies of America. While the object itself was important, the monetary "waste" that was used to purchase it was equally significant. For Black people, the use of excess money, even if it was only a few pennies on a piece of carnival glass to display on their mantel, signified to the public both their participation in consumer culture and their own desire to belong to the middle class (Mullins 2001, 164). These practices challenged the trope that Black people were socially inferior and "poor" by showcasing both Black purchasing power and genteel taste.

While capitalism created the ideology that social mobility was possible, in reality white middle-class Americans viewed the upward progress of the working classes, particularly Black people, as a challenge to their hegemony. Black people's consumption threatened white society because the objects they purchased were a form of cultural capital that projected refinement and taste. In the nineteenth and twentieth centuries, Black people's aspirations to join the middle class created fears within white society that a Black middle class would erode the distinctiveness of the white middle class (Mullins 1999a, 188–189). Despite white people's attempts to deny Black people's participation in the consumer marketplace by ensuring that they had access only to the lowest-paying jobs and by blocking their access to stores through segregation laws, Black people were able to navigate the market and became savvy consumers. Black consumers understood the transformative power of commodity consumption as a medium of identity construction and contestation of racism.

An example of Black middle-class identity construction can be seen in Megan E. Springate and Amy Raes's (2013) work at the Mann Site in former Deckertown, a predominantly white town that is now Sussex Borough, New Jersey. The Mann family owned a quarter-acre property there from 1862 to 1901. William and Louisa Mann lived in their home with their three children (who had all passed away by 1875); William's mother, Catherine; his brother, Wilson; and his uncle and grandmother (Springate and Raes 2013, 10–11). Springate and Raes discuss the public and private displays the Manns used to emphasize their middle-class status and identity. They included converting the one-and-a-half story home to a full two stories in the 1880s, buying commercially canned foods rather than canning at home, and purchasing costly ceramic wares.

White people have used legal, economic, and social obstacles to block Black people's access to property ownership in the United States because it is a mark of middle-class identity. The Manns' ownership of a home in a predominantly white town that they added to exemplifies their economic power. Evidence suggests that before 1886, the year that William became a sexton at the local, mostly white Presbyterian church, the Manns were canning at home to preserve some of their food. However, after William secured the higher-paid position the family began consuming more commercially canned foods. Springate and Raes (2013, 18, 23) suggest that this transition might have reflected either the Manns' increase in economic capital and/or a display of the family's middle-class status.

The Manns began purchasing "white granite, transfer-printed, flow-blue plates, platters, and tea wares" at the same time that the family stopped canning food at home (Springate and Raes 2013, 21). While there is some variability in the ceramic wares, perhaps because the family purchased the items one at a time, Springate and Raes (2013, 21–22) note that the Manns attempted to find wares that looked similar enough to what they had that it looked like they had matching sets.

The Manns had more economic capital to use for renovating their home than the residents of Timbuctoo did. As we have seen, the Davis's small plot and small house built with substandard materials indicate a family negotiating a life of poverty. But both the Manns and residents of Timbuctoo understood how consumer culture display could be used to create their own identity and desire to become members of the middle class. However, because of their economic means, the Manns were able to display their wealth through more accepted forms of middle-class identity, such as making additions to their home, relying less on home canning, and purchasing more expensive tableware. In contrast, because their resources were more limited, the Davises and other residents of Timbuctoo could participate in middle-class consumerism only with carefully selected, inexpensive consumer goods.

While the residents of Timbuctoo had to cope with poverty, they were also active social agents who operated within a broader capitalist society that emphasized individualism and social mobility. Yet through collective action they formed a close-knit community whose members supported each other. As one elder remembers:

> So we came up the hard way. And I always say I know what it is to have, and I know what it is not to have, and I appreciate where I came from. . . . I know when I was coming up, we were poor of course, and every time I wanted a pair of shoes or a dress, someone would give my mother some clothes, and I said Lord if I ever got grown, I'm going to have all the clothes I want, all the shoes I want, because I got tired of hand-me-downs. But as I got older I found out that was the lord making a way for my mother and father because you know they weren't

able to afford it so I look back on where I came and I thank god and
I appreciate everything that I did. (quoted in Barton et al. 2013, 134)

The residents of Timbuctoo were socialized into understanding the power
of objects as constructors of identity that could contest the labeling of inferiority. More important, the residents of Timbuctoo used display objects
such as bric-a-brac as media to project and construct their own desires
and aspirations. Documentary and archaeological evidence suggest that
many of the residents were on the lower end of the economic spectrum.
For these residents, purchasing bric-a-brac, no matter how inexpensive,
still represented a monetary investment that challenged narratives of poverty and consumption. In the most traditional sense, bric-a-brac and other
display objects served no immediate functional value, and members of
the larger society might consider that spending money on such items was
whimsical or irrational. However, consumerism should not be understood
as a dialectic between the rational and irrational. Rather, consumption op-
erates through decisions that are made through different filters of socialized habitus (Sassatelli 2007, 53). Simply because bric-a-brac did not have
a utilitarian function does not mean that such items were not meaningful
objects for the owners. For marginalized peoples, bric-a-brac embodied the
aspirations of individual identity and upward social mobility. These objects
were used to construct identities of genteel refinement despite the owners'
lack of economic capital. While many of the residents of Timbuctoo had
to endure the realities of economic marginalization, they still were well socialized in the networks of consumer culture and understood the dynamic
power of material culture.

8

CONCLUSION

This book has delved into the dynamic nature of archaeology at Timbuctoo, where the archaeological record was heavily influenced by the confluence of race and class. These pervasive social structures affected the ability of many residents to acquire cultural, economic, social, and symbolic capital in the context of multidimensional networks of power. Persevering in a racialized and class-oriented society required many Black people to develop and depend on a distinct habitus, or worldview, that both enabled and restricted their individual practice. This book interprets the practices of marginalized individuals and groups as improvisational actions that they developed from their experience of living on the social and economic periphery. Yard sweeping, using adaptive building methods such as inferior bricks, home canning, and the savvy negotiation of the consumer market were the practices of individuals who were socialized at the intersection of race and class. However, characterizing the archaeological record of Timbuctoo as merely a reflection of poverty fails to convey the residents' power to use material culture to contest the dominant white view that they were "poor" and to construct their own desires. This interpretation complicates the narrative of Timbuctoo by emphasizing the racialized and class-based repression that influenced the daily lives of residents while also conveying that they were active social agents who understood the symbolism of objects as both reflectors and constructors of collective and individual identities.

This concluding chapter places the history and archaeology of Timbuctoo in the context of the archaeological scholarship on other Black communities in New Jersey. Doing so situates Timbuctoo in the broader archaeological discourse of African America. These comparisons show how Black communities shared behaviors and practices that pushed back against economic, political, and social marginalization.

Limited archaeological work had been done on Black communities in New Jersey. Expanding our comparisons to sites outside the state is fraught with shortcomings, particularly because New Jersey's history on racial issues is complex. It was both institutionally against Black people's rights and yet individuals within the state were progressive, as seen in the examples of Quaker actions against slavery. New Jersey is unique, and any in-depth comparisons to Black communities outside the state would be anecdotal at best and inaccurate at worst (Springate and Raes 2013, 12).

To date, only two nineteenth-century Black communities in New Jersey have been surveyed: Saddlertown in Camden County and Skunk Hollow in Bergen County. Saddlertown is less than 20 miles away from Timbuctoo in Haddon Township. The community was founded in the 1830s by Joshua Saddler, a former slave from Maryland (Wieczorek and Grzybowski 2008, 21). Like Timbuctoo, Saddlertown was located near a Quaker stronghold, Haddonfield, and is also thought to have been a station on the Underground Railroad. Also as was the case at Timbuctoo, the residents of Saddlertown could get only low-wage jobs or work in domestic service for white Quakers. The aboveground remains of the community were destroyed by suburban sprawl in the 1950s (22).

Scott Wieczorek and Susan Grzybowski of Louis Berger Group completed limited fieldwork at Saddlertown prior to the restoration of the Saddler's Run watershed. Their work was limited to two project areas (Work Zones 11 and 16) that could be affected by the restoration project (Wieczorek and Grzybowski 2008, i). Work Zone 11, the John Saddler Site, was a dwelling that dated to the period 1857–1932. John Saddler was a direct descendant of the community's founder. Twenty-eight shovel test pits were excavated near the Saddler home and a total of 371 artifacts was recovered from the site. Of these, 64.1 percent was related to the kitchen (tablewares and utensils), 31.2 percent consisted of architectural materials, and 4.5 percent consisted of small finds. The mean date for the assemblage was 1884 (Wieczorek and Grzybowski 2008, 72–73).

The survey at Work Zone 16, Saddler's Wood Site, was an open area that dated from 1857 to the 1950s. Surface and subsurface surveys of the site recovered 366 artifacts (82.2 percent was related to kitchens, 13.7 percent consisted of architectural materials, and 3.9 percent consisted of small finds). The mean date for the assemblage was 1931. The interpretation of the archaeology of Saddlertown is similar to my interpretation of the archaeology of Timbuctoo in two ways: it was located near a Quaker population and its members were economically marginalized.

Home canning paraphernalia dating from the late nineteenth to the early twentieth centuries suggests that the residents of Saddlertown, like those of Timbuctoo, preserved food at home. Although this practice was quite common for the era, situating it in the historical and archaeological context of an impoverished Black community emphasizes that people canned food so they could feed their families in the winter and early spring as a way of increasing food security. Archaeologists have identified the practice of putting up, or canning surplus food, in other Black communities (Wilkie 2000, 124–126; Palmer 2011, 151) and in other socially and economically marginalized communities (Wood 2002).

The Saddlertown assemblage also includes evidence that the residents purchased commercially canned foods. Again, this consumer behavior was common, as evidence from many nineteenth- and twentieth-century sites has shown. However, looking at it through the lens of poverty reveals insights into marginalized people's lives. For example, in her examination of the foodways of ethnically diverse white coal miner families in Berwind, Colorado, Margaret Wood (2002, 180–181) noted a growing dependence on commercially canned foods in the period 1900 to 1910. She attributed this to the increased domestic responsibilities of women who were taking in boarders. More boarders meant more work, resulting in less time for home canning (Wood 2002, 180–181).

However, Wood (2002, 362–363) reported that during periods of economic uncertainty, home canning increased. Whether they consumed commercially canned foods to save on time and energy or canned food at home to increase food security, what we see are the savvy practices of people who lived in poverty.

The nineteenth-century Black community that lived at Skunk Hollow, New Jersey, had a similar pattern of responses to systemic poverty. Founded in 1806, Skunk Hollow was located in the Palisades region of rural northeastern New Jersey. The impoverished community was populated by formerly enslaved and freeborn people. Like the residents of Timbuctoo, residents of Skunk Hollow were targeted by slave catchers and lived with systemic racism (Geismar 1982, 193–194). As the need for a protected community decreased after slavery ended, the population declined. By 1905, Skunk Hollow had been abandoned (Geismar 1982, 37).

Archaeologist Joan Geismar surveyed the community in 1978. She did surface collection and shovel testing around twenty-one structures (Geismar 1982, 92). Tax records and archaeological evidence suggest that while the residents at Skunk Hollow were on the lower end of the economic spectrum in the first half of the nineteenth century, they were economically better off than residents of other early nineteenth-century Black communities (Geismar 1982, 193–194). However, Geismar notes that after the death of Rev. William Thompson, the community's leader, in 1886, the economic status of Skunk Hollow residents declined.

Archaeologists recovered a total of 11,892 artifacts from Skunk Hollow. Geismar separated the artifacts into ten categories: leather (6.1 percent), faunal remains (6.1 percent), coal (2.8 percent), plaster fragments (4.6 percent), bricks (2.2 percent), glass fragments (48 percent), ceramics (4.8 percent), metal fragments (16 percent), miscellaneous (0.8 percent), and general miscellany (1.1 percent). Geismar based her interpretation on a social disintegration model to explain how the community's decline was linked to the death of Rev. Thompson.[1]

Similar to what the evidence shows at Timbuctoo and Saddlertown, there is evidence that people at Skunk Hollow lived in poverty from 1806 to 1911. Of particular interest to our discussion is Geismar's (1982, 124–127) interpretation of the bricks from Skunk Hollow. A total of 264 whole bricks and brick fragments was recovered from the site. The majority were poorly constructed and had considerable variation in size, density, and color. Geismar argued the bricks were either made locally or were purchased from nearby brickyards. Fieldwork indicated that the bricks were used only for chimneys and not for foundations. Geismar (1982, 125) argued that this was because bricks were expensive and the builders wanted to save money when they built chimneys. She also noted that many of the bricks had probably been removed from abandoned structures and reused (Geismar 1982, 127). Recycling inferior-quality bricks and using bricks of varied quality is similar to what we found at Timbuctoo.

Containers for commercially processed food, including those labeled Mellin's Infant Food that date from 1888 to 1898, were also recovered from Skunk Hollow. Geismar (1982, 139–140) argues that the presence of Mellin's Infant Food suggests that some households had the economic resources to purchase commercially canned baby food for convenience, but some working mothers may have bought it because it was cost-effective. I would add, following the examples that we have seen from Wood's (2002) work at Berwind, that working mothers may have chosen to buy commercially processed food to save time and energy.

The consistent characteristic of nineteenth- and twentieth-century Black archaeological sites is the largely marginalized economic and social status of the residents. Racism made it difficult for most Black people to acquire economic, political, and social capital in the nineteenth and early twentieth centuries. As a result of economic, political, and social structural obstacles, many Black people had to improvise in their everyday practice. Thus, the archaeological record throughout much of Black America reflects practices that improvised with limited resources. My review of archaeological scholarship on Black community sites that date to the mid-nineteenth to early twentieth centuries found that artifact assemblages consist of mostly inexpensive objects that are often of low quality. While it is obvious that people who have been racialized and kept in poverty by structural obstacles would consume lower-cost commodities and make the most of their limited resources, these people also actively pushed back against repression. Black people did not simply seek out consumer goods based on on-the-spot decisions; they made decisions that made the most of what they had. These decisions were based on a habitus, a worldview, of "making do."

What is also apparent in my review of archaeological literature is that while the vast majority of items in artifact assemblages are indicative of poverty, they are punctuated by highly symbolic objects such as bric-a-brac. Black people acquired these objects to contest pejorative social attitudes toward them and to project individual desire. The growth of consumer culture in the late nineteenth century created a flood of inexpensive, yet socially powerful objects that middle- and working-class consumers were all too happy to consume. These reflexive and discursive relationships between people and objects altered the ways in which people identified with one another and within themselves.

The confluence of racism and economic marginalization has been well documented in the archaeological records of nineteenth- and twentieth-century African America (Orser 1998, 2004, 2007; Mullins 1999a, 2011; Wilkie 2000; Leone et al. 2005; Barnes 2011). While much of the early archaeological scholarship on Black sites in the United States focused on the recovery of cultural continuities, more recently there has been a push to understand race and its intersectionality with social and economic class. Black agency is not limited to the syncretism of ritual practices rooted in West African spirituality manifested in a select handful of artifacts. Instead, it is revealed in a contextual approach that seeks to understand the structural disposition and everyday meanings constructed in the archaeological records (Orser 2004, 119).

Central to grasping this intertwined relationship between race and class is understanding how individual practices were developed through a learned habitus of marginalization and perseverance. But we must also understand that the residents of Timbuctoo also operated in a capitalist society that emphasized individuality, social mobility, and desire. These ideologies were driving factors not only for African Americans but also for the other working classes who struggled with the illusion that they could belong to the American middle class.

While producing, advertising, and consuming commodities created the illusion of middle-class membership for impoverished people like the residents of Timbuctoo, consumerism offered them the ability to construct their own identity to contest the label that they were "poor." The archaeological analysis of people who lived in poverty during the nineteenth and twentieth centuries involves trying to understand the perceived common-sense practices of enduring poverty in the context of the equally perceived impracticality of buying symbolic objects. The consumption and display of a Depression glass plate has as much *function* as the reuse of a home canning jar does. While the canning jar provides preserved food, the displayed plate projects the identity and aspirations of its owner. Although each artifact type is demonstrably different, each serves an equally important role for the individual.

Discussion

This book is not the final word on historical and archaeological study at Timbuctoo; it is only one interpretation. When I talk to the present-day community about the history and archaeology of Timbuctoo, I focus on how its residents resisted, persevered, and triumphed over adversity. But the struggle is not over, as people of color continue to be the targets of structural and everyday forms of racist repression. In 2020, Black Lives Matter protests around the world called out systemic poverty, mass incarceration, police brutality, and racism. While many archaeologists may feel that their work has little bearing on social activism, archaeology does have power. It has the power to study the legacies of repression and to challenge the manifestations of racism we see today (see, for example, Barton 2021).

It is particularly important to focus on issues that relate to people of color. Archaeologists are uniquely equipped to use a diverse arsenal of methods to research the past, inform the present, and create praxis that works toward a more equitable future for marginalized peoples. It is my belief that collaborating with descendant communities as equal partners is the most fruitful, most meaningful action archaeologists can take. I believe that we are public servants to the communities who are connected to sites like Timbuctoo, and in our service to those communities, we must address the issues that are important to them.

Our work at Timbuctoo challenged the authorized public memory that presented New Jersey's history as a narrative of racial harmony and opportunity. Even though many Quakers lived in New Jersey who were proponents of abolition and *some* Black social rights in the North in the nineteenth century, the state was rife with structural racism and repression.

After the end of slavery, residents of places like Timbuctoo, Saddlertown, and Skunk Hollow continued to experience segregation, social and economic repression, and even confrontations with the Ku Klux Klan.

Racial injustice in New Jersey has not ended. For example, in 2019, 15.8 percent of New Jersey's Black population was living below the poverty line, compared to only 5.6 percent of the white population.[2] Additionally, although they constitute only 14 percent of the total population, African Americans account for 61 percent of the prison population in the state (Vera Institute of Justice 2019, 1). African Americans are twelve times more likely to be incarcerated than white people in the state. Racial profiling, biased prosecutors, and resistance to criminal justice reform have made New Jersey the nation's leader for carceral racial disparities (The Fund for New Jersey 2019, 2). These are only a few examples of the continued struggles that Black New Jerseyans face in the present day. The good news is that through social activism and progressive political action, New Jersey is beginning to address economic equity and criminal justice reform. However, the fight is not over, as the structural racism Black people endured in the past has legacies that negatively affect people today. This archaeological project may have only a limited impact on modern structures of racism and classism, but it is a start. We can use our craft, the study of the material culture of the past, to create positive change in the present day.

Moreover, people in the past were not limited to one identity but were able to construct their own desires and aspirations through material culture and consumerism. The same is true today. In our society, the role of objects can be either overemphasized so that material culture seems like the sole identifier for people or it can be so understated that objects are seen as merely things that have no bearing on our lives. But objects are important:

they both reflect and reproduce the values, beliefs, and practices of our society. The archaeology at Timbuctoo is a story of how people used the landscape, consumer culture, and their own resourcefulness to empower themselves in the face of continued repression. The lessons and themes from this story reverberate today, as communities of color continue to struggle against racism. If my years of research and my countless conversations with community members at Timbuctoo have taught me anything, it is that the human spirit perseveres and that people continue to rage against the systems that oppress them and continue to fight for social justice. This is a war that archaeologists must wage on behalf of the people we study in the past and on behalf of our brothers and sisters in the present.

NOTES

Chapter 2. The Intersectionality of Race and Class

1. "Charlottesville: Race and Terror," *Vice News,* August 21, 2017, accessed August 12, 2020, https://www.vice.com/en/article/qvzn8p/vice-news-tonight-full-episode-charlottesville-race-and-terror; David Neiwert, "Explaining 'You Will Not Replace Us,' 'Blood and Soil,' 'Russia Is Our Friend,' and Other Catchphrases from Torch-Bearing Marchers in Charlottesville," *Southern Poverty Law Center,* October 10, 2017, https://www.splcenter.org/hatewatch/2017/10/10/when-white-nationalists-chant-their-weird-slogans-what-do-they-mean.

2. Eyder Peralta, "Supreme Court Upholds University of Texas' Affirmative Action Program," *National Public Radio,* June 23, 2016, accessed July 1, 2020, https://www.npr.org/sections/thetwo-way/2016/06/23/483228011/supreme-court-upholds-university-of-texas-affirmative-action-program.

3. "'Welfare Queen' Becomes Issue in Reagan Campaign," *New York Times,* February 15, 1976, https://timesmachine.nytimes.com/timesmachine/1976/02/15/113445299.html?pageNumber=51.

4. Donald J. Trump, presidential campaign speech, Phoenix, Arizona, July 11, 2015, YouTube video, https://www.youtube.com/watch?v=rDtvk9GRrpQ.

5. Amy Gardner, Kate Rabinowitz, and Harry Stevens, "How GOP-Backed Voting Measures Could Create Hurdles for Tens of Millions of Voters," *Washington Post,* March 11, 2021, https://www.washingtonpost.com/politics/interactive/2021/voting-restrictions-republicans-states/.

Chapter 3. History of Timbuctoo

1. Henry L. Gates Jr., *Wonders of the World: Road to Timbuktu,* documentary film (New York: Public Broadcasting Service. 1999).

2. "Trouble among the Darkies," *New Jersey Mirror,* April 15, 1858.

3. *An Act for the Gradual Abolition of Slavery . . . Passed at Trenton, February 15, 1804* (Burlington, [N. J.]: S. C. Ustick, 1804), https://www.loc.gov/item/rbpe.0990100b/.

4. "Trouble among the Darkies."

5. "Excitement at Timbuctoo, the Battle of Pine Swamp: The Invaders Forced to Retreat," *New Jersey Mirror,* December 6, 1860.

6. "12,000 of Klan Out at Jersey Meeting: Hold Heavily Guarded Initiation on a Lonely Farm Near New Brunswick," *New York Times,* May 3, 1923.

7. "Kloran or Ritual of the WKKK," *New York Times,* August 19, 1923.

Chapter 4. Landscapes of Timbuctoo

1. "Timbuctoo," *New Jersey Mirror,* June 21, 1855.

2. "The Colored Camping Meeting at Timbuctoo," *The Morning Post,* September 2, 1886.

3. Ray Berry, "The Real Reason for Sweeping Yards Is Snakes," letter to the editor, *New York Times,* August 22, 1993.

Chapter 5. The Davis Home

1. The term wet clamp refers to the technique of using unfired bricks to make a self-contained kiln.

Chapter 6. Food, Strife, and Preservation

1. "Peanut Butter or Steak?" *Weekly News Letter,* July 24, 1918, 12.

Chapter 7. Display and Desire

1. The consumer choice model focuses on the connections between artifact types and "socioeconomic" status. This model has largely fallen out of favor because it fails to account for individual agency.

Chapter 8. Conclusion

1. Social disintegration is a research model used to explain the decline of a community due to the breakdown of social traditions and practices over time.

2. Vinetta Kapahi, "Census 2019: Poverty in New Jersey Remains Higher Than Pre-Recession Levels," New Jersey Policy Perspective, September 24, 2020, https://www.njpp.org/publications/blog-category/census-2019-poverty-in-new-jersey-remains-higher-than-pre-recession-levels/.

REFERENCE LIST

Adirondack History Center. 2002. *Dreaming of Timbuctoo*. Elizabethtown, NY: Adirondack History Center.

Althusser, Louis. 1971. *Lenin and Philosophy and Other Essays*. New York: Monthly Review Press.

Astle, Gail. 2008. Memorial Day Eulogy at Timbuctoo Cemetery in Westampton Township, New Jersey. Rancocas, NJ, website, May 25, 2008. Accessed June 13, 2019. http://rancocasvillagenj.org/wths_reference/timbuctoo-memorial/.

Atalay, Sonya. 2012. *Community-Based Archaeology: Research with, by and for Indigenous and Local Communities*. Berkeley: University of California Press.

Barnes, Jodi A. 2011. *The Materiality of Freedom: Archaeologies of Postemancipation Life*. Columbia: University of South Carolina.

Barton, Christopher P. 2012. Tacking between Black and White: The Archaeology of Race Relations in Gilded Age Philadelphia. In "Gilded Age Archaeologies: Archaeological Explorations of Our Times." Special issue, *International Journal of Historical Archaeology* 16(4): 634–650.

———. 2013. Identity and Improvisation: Archaeology at the African American Community of Timbuctoo, NJ. PhD diss., Temple University, Philadelphia, PA.

———, ed. 2021. *Trowels in the Trenches: Archaeology as Social Activism*. Gainesville: University Press of Florida.

Barton, Christopher P., and Patricia Markert. 2012. Collaborative Archaeology, Oral History and Social Memory at Timbuctoo, NJ. *Journal of African Diaspora Archaeology and Heritage* 1(1): 79–102.

Barton, Christopher P., Patricia Markert, and David G. Orr. 2013. *Archaeological Investigation of the Davis Site, Timbuctoo, Westampton, Burlington County, New Jersey*. Site report prepared for Westampton Township.

Barton, Christopher P., and Kyle Somerville. 2012. Play Things: Children's Racialized Mechanical Banks and Toys, 1880–1930. *International Journal of Historical Archaeology* 16(1): 47–85.

———. 2016. *Historical Racialized Toys in the United States*. New York: Routledge.

Battle-Baptiste, Whitney. 2010. Sweepin' Spirits: Power and Transformation on the Plantation Landscape. In *The Archaeology and Preservation of Gendered Landscapes*, edited by Sherene Baugher and Suzanne Spencer-Wood, 81–94. New York: Springer.

———. 2011. *Black Feminist Archaeology.* Walnut Creek, CA: Left Coast Press.

Beaudry, Mary C., and Ellen P. Berkland. 2007. The Archaeology of the African Meeting House on Nantucket. In *Archaeology of Atlantic Africa and African Diaspora,* edited by Akinwumi Ogundiran and Toyin Falola, 395–412. Bloomington: Indiana University Press.

Belk, Russell W. 1988. Possessions and the Extended Self. *Journal of Consumer Research* 15(2): 139–168.

Bentley, Amy. 1998. *Eating for Victory: Food Rationing and the Politics of Domesticity.* Urbana: University of Illinois Press.

Bitting, A. W., and K. G. Bitting. 1916. *Canning and How to Use Canned Foods.* Washington, DC: National Capital Press.

Bonilla-Silva, Eduardo. 1997. Rethinking Racism: Toward a Structural Interpretation. *American Sociological Review* 62(3): 465–480.

Bourdieu, Pierre. 1977. *Outline of a Theory of Practice.* New York: Cambridge University Press.

———. 1986. The Forms of Capital. In *Handbook of Theory and Research for the Sociology of Education,* edited by J. Richardson, 241–258. New York: Greenwood.

———. 1984. *Social Distinction: A Social Critique of the Judgment of Taste.* New York: Harvard University Press.

———. 1990. *The Logic of Practice.* Stanford, CA: Stanford University Press.

Brandon, James C., and James M. Davidson. 2005. The Landscape of Van Winkle's Mill: Identity, Myth, and Modernity in the Ozark Upland South. *Historical Archaeology* 39(3): 113–131.

Brown, Frank. 2004. Nixon's "Southern Strategy" and Forces Against Brown. *The Journal of Negro Education* 73(3): 191–208.

Brown, Glenn. 1885. *Healthy Foundations for Houses.* New York: D. Van Nostrand.

Bruère, Martha B., and Robert W. Bruère. 1912. *Increasing Home Efficiency.* New York: MacMillan Company.

Cabak, Melanie A., Mark Groover, and Mary M. Inkrot. 1999. Rural Modernization during the Recent Past: Farmstead Archaeology in the Aiken Plateau. *Historical Archaeology* 33(4): 19–43.

Cadbury, Henry. 1936. Negro Membership in the Society of Friends. *Journal of Negro History* 21(1): 151–213.

Cerroni-Long, E. L. 1987. Benign Neglect?: Anthropology and the Study of Blacks in the United States. *Journal of Black Studies* 17(4): 438–459.

Chadwick, William, and Peter Leach. 2009. *Geophysical Survey of Timbuctoo, NJ.* West Chester, PA: John Milner and Associates.

Chesney, Sarah Jane. 2014. The Fruits of Their Labors: Exploring William Hamilton's Greenhouse Complex and the Rise of American Botany in Early Federal Philadelphia. Ph.D. diss., College of William and Mary, Williamsburg, VA.

Churchill, Allen L., and Leonard Wickenden. 1923. *The House-Owner's Book: A Manual for the Helpful Guidance of Those Who Are Interested in the Building or Conduct of Homes.* New York: Funk and Wagnalls Company.

Clark, T. M. 1895. *Building Superintendence: A Manual for Young Architects, Students and*

Others Interested in Building Operations as Carried on at the Present Day. London: MacMillan Company.

Cocroft, Susanna. 1912. *Foods: Nutrition and Digestion.* Chicago: Physical Culture Extension Society.

Collins, Gail. 2003. *America's Women: 400 Years of Dolls, Drudges, Helpmates, and Heroines.* New York: William Morrow Paperbacks.

Collins, James H. 1924. *The Story of Canned Foods.* New York: E. P. Dutton & Company.

Condit, Elizabeth, and Jessie A. Long. 1914. *How to Cook and Why.* New York: Harper & Brothers.

Cook, Lauren J., Rebecca Yamin, and John P. McCarthy. 1996. Shopping as Meaningful Action: Toward a Redefinition of Consumption in Historical Archaeology. *Historical Archaeology* 30(4): 50–65.

Cross, Gary S. 2000. *An All-Consuming Century: Why Commercialism Won in Modern America.* New York: Columbia University Press.

Davidson, James M. 2007. "Resurrection Men" in Dallas: The Illegal Use of Black Bodies as Medical Cadavers (1999–1907). *International Journal of Historical Archaeology* 11(3): 193–220.

Davidson, James, Erika Roberts, and Clete Rooney. 2006. Excavations at Kingsley Plantation, Florida. *African Diaspora Archaeology Newsletter* (September). http://www.diaspora.illinois.edu/news0906/news0906.html#2.

Davis, Charles T. 1895. *A Practical Treatise on Brick, Tiles and Terra-Cotta.* Philadelphia, PA: Henry Carey Baird & Co.

De Certeau, Michel. 1984. *The Practice of Everyday Life.* Berkeley: University of California Press.

De Cunzo, Lu Ann. 2004. *A Historical Archaeology of Delaware: People, Contexts, and the Cultures of Agriculture.* Knoxville: University of Tennessee Press.

Deetz, James. 1996. *In Small Things Forgotten: An Archaeology of Early American Life.* New York: Anchor Books.

Delle, James A. 2008. A Tale of Two Tunnels: Memory, Archaeology, and the Underground Railroad. *Journal of Social Archaeology* 8(1): 64–94.

Dickson, Maxcy R. 1944. *The Food Front in World War I.* Washington, DC: American Council on Public Affairs.

Diemer, Andrew. 2009. Reconstructing Philadelphia: African Americans and Politics in the Post–Civil War North. *Pennsylvania Magazine of History and Biography* 113(1): 29–58.

Douglass, Frederick. 1849. *Narrative of the Life of Frederick Douglass an American Slave.* Boston: The Antislavery Office.

Du Bois, W. E. B. 1935. *Black Reconstruction in America.* Cleveland: Harcourt Brace.

Dubois, Felix. 1896. *Timbuctoo the Mysterious.* Trans. Diana White. New York: Longmans, Green and Co.

Echo-Hawk, Roger, and Larry J. Zimmerman. 2006. Beyond Racism: Some Opinions about Racialism and American Archaeology. *American Indian Quarterly* 30(3/4): 461–485.

Epperson, Terrence W. 1994. The Politics of Empiricism and the Construction of Race as an Analytical Category. *Transforming Anthropology* 5(1): 15–19.

———. 1999. The Contested Commons: Archaeologies of Race, Repression, and Resistance in New York City. In *Historical Archaeologies of Capitalism,* edited by Mark P. Leone and Parker Potter, 81–110. New York: Kluwer Academic.

Ferguson, Leland G. 1992. *Uncommon Ground: Archaeology and Early African America, 1650–1800.* Washington, DC: Smithsonian Press.

Fishman, George. 1997. *The African American Struggle for Freedom and Equality: The Development of a People's Identity, New Jersey, 1624–1850.* New York: Garland Publishing.

Fitts, Robert K. 1999. The Archaeology of Middle-Class Domesticity and Gentility in Victorian Brooklyn. *Historical Archaeology* 33: 39–62.

Fund for New Jersey, The. 2019. *Criminal Justice Reform: Reducing Mass Incarceration Would Benefit New Jersey Communities.* Princeton, NJ: The Fund for New Jersey.

Gall, Michael, Adam Heinrich, Ilene Grossman-Bailey, Philip A. Hayden, and Justine McKnight. 2020. The Place beyond the Fence: Slavery and Cultural Invention on a Delaware Tenant Farm. *Historical Archaeology* 54(2): 305–333.

Gara, Larry. 1961. *The Liberty Line: The Legend of the Underground Railroad.* Lexington: University Press of Kentucky.

Geismar, Joan H. 1982. *The Archaeology of Social Disintegration in Skunk Hollow: A Nineteenth-Century Rural Black Community.* New York: Academic Press.

Giddens, Anthony. 1979. *Central Problems in Social Theory: Action, Structure and Contradiction in Social Analysis.* Berkeley: University of California Press.

———. 1991. *Modernity and Self-Identity: Self and Society in the Late Modern Age.* Stanford, CA: Stanford University Press.

Gigantino, James J., II. 2014. *The Ragged Road to Abolition: Slavery and Freedom in New Jersey.* Philadelphia: University of Pennsylvania Press.

González-Tennant, Edward. 2014. The "Color" of Heritage: Decolonizing Collaborative Archaeology in the Caribbean. *Journal of African Diaspora Archaeology and Heritage* 3(1): 26–50.

Goode, Judith G., and Jeff Maskovsky. 2002. *The New Poverty Studies: The Ethnography of Power, Politics, and Impoverished People in the United States.* New York: NYU Press.

Gould, Elise. 2020. State of Working America Wages 2019. Economic Policy Institute. February 20. epi.org/publication/swa-wages-2019/.

Gould, Stephen Jay. 1996. *The Mismeasure of Man.* New York: W. W. Norton & Company.

Green, Harvey. 1992. *The Uncertainty of Everyday Life, 1915–1945.* New York: HarperCollins.

Gummere, Amelia M. 1922. *The Journal and Essays of John Woolman.* New York: Macmillan.

Gundaker, Grey, and Judith McWillie. 2004. *Space Hidden: The Spirit of African American Yard Work.* Knoxville: University of Tennessee Press.

Gurcke, Karl. 1987. *Bricks and Brickmaking: A Handbook for Historical Archaeology.* Moscow: University of Idaho.

Heath, B. J., and A. Bennett. 2000. "The Little Spots Allow'd Them": The Archaeological Study of African-American Yards. *Historical Archaeology* 34(2): 38–55.

Henderson, Peter. 1887. *Gardening for Pleasure: A Guide to the Amateur in the Fruit, Vegetable, and Flower Garden, with Full Directions for the Greenhouse, Conservatory, and Window Garden.* New York: O. Judd Co.

Herman, Bernard L., Susan A. Mulcahey, Rebecca J. (Sheppard) Siders, Gabrielle M. Lanier, and Nancy K. Ziegler. 1990. *Adaptation of Bungalows in the Lower Peninsula/Cypress Swamp Zone of Delaware, 1880–1940.* Newark: Center for Historic Architecture and Engineering, University of Delaware.

Hodges, George R. 1997. *Slavery and Freedom in the Rural North: African Americans in Monmouth County, New Jersey, 1665–1865.* Madison, [NJ]: Madison House Publishers.

Hoffman, Kelly M., Sophie Trawalter, Jordan R. Axt, and M. Norman Oliver. 2016. Racial Bias in Pain Assessment and Treatment Recommendations, and False Beliefs about Biological Differences between Blacks and Whites. *Psychological and Cognitive Sciences* 113(16): 4296–4301.

Hughes, Mary B. 1918. *Every Woman's Canning Book: The ABC of Safe Home Canning by the Cold Pack Method.* Boston: Whitecomb & Barrons.

Hunter, Lynette. 1989. Nineteenth- and Twentieth-Century Trends in Food Preserving: Frugality, Nutrition or Luxury. In *"Waste Not, Want Not": Food Preservation from Early Times to the Present Day,* edited by Anne C. Wilson, 134–158. Edinburgh: Edinburgh University Press.

Ignatiev, Noel. 1995. *How the Irish Became White.* New York: Routledge.

Interracial Committee, New Jersey Department of Institutions and Agencies. 1932. *Survey of Negro Life in New Jersey.* Newark, NJ: Conference of Social Work.

Jackson, Kellie Carter. 2019. *Force and Freedom: Black Abolitionists and the Politics of Violence.* Philadelphia: University of Pennsylvania Press.

Jenkins, Virginia Scott. 1994. *The Lawn: A History of an American Obsession.* New York: Smithsonian Books.

Jones, Robert P., Daniel Cox, and Rachel Lienesch. 2017. Beyond Economics: Fears of Cultural Displacement Pushed the White Working Class to Trump. PRRI/The Atlantic Report. https://www.prri.org/research/white-working-class-attitudes-economy-trade-immigration-election-donald-trump/.

Jonsson-Rose, Nils. 1897. *Lawns and Gardens: How to Plant and Beautify the Home Lot, the Pleasure Ground, and Garden.* New York: G. P. Putnam's Sons.

Kelly, David H. 1991. Egyptians and Ethiopians: Color, Race, and Racism. *The Classical Outlook* 68(3): 77–82.

Kelso, William M. 1984. *Kingsmill Plantations, 1619–1800: Archaeology of Country Life in Colonial Virginia.* Charlottesville: University of Virginia Press.

Klinghoffer, Judith A., and Lois Elkis. 1992. "The Petticoat Electors": Women's Suffrage in New Jersey, 1776–1807. *Early Republic* 12(2): 159–193.

Krampner, Jon. 2013. *Creamy & Crunchy: An Informal History of Peanut Butter, the All-American Food.* New York: University of Columbia Press.

LaRoche, Cheryl J. 2014. *Free Black Communities and the Underground Railroad: The Geography of Resistance.* Chicago: University of Illinois Press.

LaRoche, Cheryl J., and Michael L. Blakey. 1997. Seizing Intellectual Power: The Dialogue at the New York Burial Ground. *Historical Archaeology* 31(3): 84–106.

Laszewski, Robert. 2020. The Trump and Republican 2020 Health Care Plan. *Forbes*, January 5. https://www.forbes.com/sites/robertlaszewski2/2020/01/05/the-trump-and-republican-health-care-plan/?sh=32d8a20f1846.

Leonardo, Zeus. 2005. Through the Multicultural Glass: Althusser, Ideology, and Race Relations in Post–Civil Rights America. *Policy Futures in Education* 3(4): 400–412.

Leone, Mark P. 1984. Interpreting Ideology in Historical Archaeology: Using the Rules of Perspective in the William Paca Garden in Annapolis, Maryland. In *Ideology, Representation, and Power in Prehistory,* edited by C. Tilley and D. Miller, 25–25. Cambridge: Cambridge University Press.

———. 2005. *The Archaeology of Liberty in an American Capital: Excavations in Annapolis.* Berkeley: University of California Press.

———. 2010. *Critical Historical Archaeology.* Walnut Creek, CA: Left Coast Press.

Leone, Mark, Parker Potter Jr., and Paul Shackel. 1987. Toward a Critical Archaeology. *Current Anthropology* 28(3): 283–302.

Leone, Mark P., C. J. LaRoche, and J. J. Babiarz. 2005. The Archaeology of Black Americans in Recent Times. *Annual Review of Anthropology* 34: 575–598.

Linderoth, Matthew. 2010. *Prohibition on the North Jersey Shore: Gangsters on Vacation.* Charleston, SC: History Press.

Little, Barbara J., and Paul A. Shackel. 2014. *Archaeology, Heritage, and Civic Engagement: Working toward the Public Good.* Walnut Creek, CA: Left Coast Press.

Lyght, Ernest. 1978. *Path of Freedom: The Black Presence in New Jersey's Burlington County.* Cherry Hill, NJ: E and E Publishing.

Lynch, Gerard. 1994. *Brickwork: History, Technology and Practice.* London: Donhead.

MacGaffey, Wyatt. 1986. *Religion and Society in Central Africa: The BaKongo of Lower Zaire.* Chicago: University of Chicago Press.

Marrin, Richard B. 2007. *Runaways of Colonial New Jersey: Indentured Servants, Slaves, Deserters, and Prisoners, 1720–1781.* Westminster: Heritage Books.

Marx, Karl, and Friedrich Engels. 2016. *The Civil War in the United States.* New York: International Publishers.

Matt, Susan J. 2003. *Keeping up with the Joneses: Envy in American Consumer Society, 1890–1930.* Philadelphia: University of Pennsylvania Press.

Matthews, Christopher N. 2012. *Archaeology of American Capitalism.* Gainesville: University of Florida Press.

———. 2020. *A Struggle for Heritage: Archaeology and Civil Rights in a Long Island Community.* Gainesville: University Press of Florida.

Mayo, James M. 1993. *The American Grocery Store: The Business Evolution of an Architectural Space.* Westport, CT: Greenwood Press.

McDaniel, Donna, and Vanessa D. Julye. 2009. *Fit for Freedom, Not for Friendship: Quakers, African Americans, and the Myth of Racial Justice.* Philadelphia: Quaker Press.

McDavid, Carol. 2002. Archaeologies That Hurt; Descendants That Matter: A Pragmatic Approach to Collaboration in the Public Interpretation of African-American Archaeology. *World Archaeology* 34(2): 303–314.

———. 2007. Beyond Strategy and Good Intentions: Archaeology, Race and White Privilege. In *Archaeology as a Tool of Civic Engagement,* edited by Barbara J. Little and Paul A. Shackel, 67–88. Lanham, MD: AltaMira Press.

McGuire, Randall H. 2008. *Archaeology as Political Action.* Berkeley: University of California Press.

Mertz, Barbara. 2008. *Red Land, Black Land: Daily Life in Ancient Egypt.* New York: Harper Collins.

Miller, Edward A. 1995. *Robert Smalls from Slavery to Congress, 1839–1915.* Columbia, SC: University of South Carolina Press.

Miller, George L. 1980. Classification and Economic Scaling of 19th Century Ceramics. *Historical Archaeology* 14(1): 1–40.

Mingus, Scott. 2016. *The Ground Swallowed Them Up: Slavery and the Underground Railroad in York County, Pa.* York, PA: York County History Center.

Mullins, Paul R. 1999a. *Race and Affluence: An Archaeology of African America and Consumer Culture.* New York: Kluwer Academic.

———. 1999b. Race and the Genteel Consumer: Class and African American Consumption, 1850–1930. *Historical Archaeology* 33(1): 22–38.

———. 2001. Racializing the Parlor: Race and Victorian Bric-a-Brac Consumption. In *Race and the Archaeology of Identity,* edited by Charles E. Orser Jr., 158–176. Salt Lake City: University of Utah Press.

———. 2011. *The Archaeology of Consumer Culture.* Gainesville: University of Florida Press.

———. 2017. Imagining Conformity: Consumption and Homogeneity in the Postwar African American Suburbs. *Historical Archaeology* 51: 88–99.

Mullins, Paul R., Modupe Labode, Lewis C. Jones, Brandon Muncy, Michael Essex, and Alex Kruse. 2011. Consuming Lines of Difference: The Politics of Wealth and Poverty along the Color Line. *Historical Archaeology* 45(3): 140–150.

Mulrooney, Margaret M. 2002. *Black Powder, White Lace: The du Pont Irish and Cultural Identity in Nineteenth-Century America.* Hanover: University of New Hampshire.

Nash, Gary B., and Jean R. Soderlund. 1991. *Freedom by Degrees: Emancipation in Pennsylvania and Its Aftermath.* New York: Oxford University Press.

National Magazine. 1917. *How to Save Money on Food: Home Canning, Preserving without Sugar, Drying Fruits, Salt Packing, Food Values as Recommended by the United States Government.* Boston: Chapple Publishing Company.

Neil, Marion H. 1914. *Canning, Preserving and Pickling.* New York: David McKay.

New Jersey State Board of Education. 1890. *Annual Report of the New Jersey State Board of Education.* Trenton, NJ: Board of Education.

———. 1897. *Annual Report of the State Board of Education and the Superintendent of Public Instruction of New Jersey.* Trenton, NJ: Board of Education.

Newman, Richard S. 2008. *Freedom's Prophet: Bishop Richard Allen, the AME Church, and the Black Founding Fathers.* New York: New York University Press.

Northup, Solomon. 1853. *Twelve Years a Slave.* Auburn, NY: Derby and Miller.

Nutting, P. Bradley. 2003. Selling Elegant Glassware during the Great Depression: A. H. Heisey & Company and the New Deal. *The Business History Review* 77(2): 447–478.

Orser, Charles E., Jr. 1988. *The Material Basis of the Postbellum Tenant Plantation: Historical Archaeology in the South Carolina Piedmont.* Athens: University of Georgia Press.

———. 1998. The Challenge of Race to American Historical Archaeology. *American Anthropologist* 100(3): 661–668.

———. 2004. *Race and Practice in Archaeological Interpretation.* Philadelphia: University of Pennsylvania Press.

———. 2007. *The Archaeology of Race and Racialization in Historic America.* Gainesville: University of Florida Press.

Orser, Charles E., Jr., ed. 2001. *Race and the Archaeology of Identity.* Salt Lake City: University of Utah Press.

Ortner, Sherrie B. 1996. *Making Gender: The Politics and Erotics of Culture.* Boston: Beacon.

———. 1999. *The Fate of "Culture": Geertz and Beyond.* Berkeley: University of California Press.

———. 2001. Commentary: Practice, Power and the Past. *Journal of Social Archaeology* 1(2): 271–278.

Otto, John S. 1980. Race and Class on Antebellum Plantations. *Archaeological Perspectives on Ethnicity in America: Afro-American and Asian American Culture History,* edited by Robert L. Schuyler, 3–13. New York: Baywood.

———. 1984. *Cannon's Point Plantation 1794–1860: Living Conditions and Status Patterns in the Old South.* Orlando: Academic Press.

Palmer, David T. 2011. Archaeology of Jim Crow–Era African American Life on Louisiana's Sugar Plantations. In *The Materiality of Freedom: Archaeologies of Postemancipation Life,* edited by Jodi A. Barnes, 136–157. Columbia: University of South Carolina Press.

Peanut Promoter. 1922. *The Peanut Promoter: The Most Unique Publication in the World.* Suffolk, VA: Lightner Publishing Corporation.

Pezzarossi, Guido. 2019. Introduction: Rethinking the Archaeology of Capitalism: Coercion, Violence, and the Politics of Accumulation. *Historical Archaeology* 53(3): 453–467.

Ponansky, Merrick. 2004. Processes of Change—A Longitudinal Ethno-Archaeological Study of a Ghanaian Village: Hani 1970–98. *African Archaeological Review* 21(1): 31–47.

Powell, George T. 1879. *Foundations and Foundation Walls, for All Classes of Buildings, Pile Driving, Building Stones & Bricks, Pier and Wall Construction, Mortars, Limes, Cements, Concretes, Stuccos, Etc.* New York: Bicknell & Comstock.

Pressly, Thomas J. 2006. The Known World of Free Black Slaveholders: A Research Note on the Scholarship of Carter G. Woodson. *Journal of African American History* 91(1): 81–87.

Reclus, Elisee. 1888. *The Earth and Its Inhabitants: Africa.* New York: D. Appleton and Company.

Ries, Heinrich, Henry B. Kummel, and George N. Knapp. 1904. *The Clays of Clay Industries of New Jersey.* Trenton, NJ: MacCrellish & Quigley.

Roediger, David R. 1991. *The Wages of Whiteness: Race and the Making of the American Working Class*. London: Verso.

———. 2019. *How Race Survived U.S. History: From Settlement and Slavery to the Eclipse of Post-Racialism*. New York: Verso.

Rorty, R. 1991. *Objectivity, Relativism, and Truth: Philosophical Papers*, Vol. 1, Cambridge: Cambridge University Press.

Rothman, Deborah L., and Ellen-Rose Savulis, eds. 2003. *Shared Spaces and Divided Places: Material Dimensions of Gender Relations and the American Historical Landscape*. Knoxville: University of Tennessee Press.

Saitta, Dean J. 2007. *Archaeology as Collective Action*. Gainesville: University of Florida Press.

Sanger, Margaret. 2010. *Margaret Sanger: An Autobiography*. Whitefish, MT: Kessinger Publishing.

Sassatelli, Roberta. 2007. *Consumer Culture: History, Theory and Politics*. London: Sage Publications.

Sawyer, Gerald. 2004. New Salem Plantation: Continuing Investigations into African Captivity on an 18th Century Plantation in Connecticut. Paper presented at the Society for Historical Archaeology Conference, Long Beach, CA, January 6.

Sayre & Fisher Co. 1895. *Catalogue of Sayre & Fisher Co. Manufacturers of Front, Enameled, Building and Fire Brick*. Baltimore, MD: Deutsch Lithographing & Printing Co.

Scheper-Hughes, Nancy. 1992. *Death without Weeping: The Violence of Everyday Life in Brazil*. Berkeley: University of California Press.

Schlereth, Thomas J. 1981. *Artifacts and the American Past*. Nashville: American Association for State & Local History.

Schopp, Paul. 2012. The Battle of Pine Swamp. Paper presented at the Memorial Day Service at Timbuctoo, Westampton, New Jersey, May 25.

Schroy, Ellen T. 2006. *Warmen's Carnival Glass: Identification and Price Guide*. 2nd ed. Iola, WI: Krause Publications.

Shackel, Paul A. 1993. *Personal Discipline and Material Culture: An Archaeology of Annapolis, Maryland, 1695–1870*. Knoxville: University of Tennessee Press.

———. 2003. *Black and White: Race, Commemoration, and the Landscape*. New York: AltaMira Press.

———. 2009. *The Archaeology of American Labor and Working-Class Life*. Gainesville: University Press of Florida.

———. 2011. *New Philadelphia: An Archaeology of Race in the Heartland*. Berkeley: University of California Press.

Sheridan, Janet L. 2013. *National Register of Historic Places Nomination: Marshalltown Historic District*. Trenton: New Jersey Historical Commission.

Shogren, Samuel. 1986. Lifeways of the Industrial Worker: The Archaeological Record—A Summary of Three Field Seasons at Blacksmith's Hill. Unpublished site report. Wilmington, DE: Hagley Museum.

Siebert, Wilbur H. 1898. *The Underground Railroad: From Slavery to Freedom*. New York: MacMillan Company.

Singleton, Theresa A., ed. 1999. "*I, too, am America*": *Archaeological Studies of African-American Life*. Charlottesville: University Press of Virginia.

Slaughter, Thomas. 2008. *The Beautiful Soul of John Woolman, Apostle of Abolition*. New York: Hill and Wang.

Smedley, Audrey. 1999. *Race in North America: Origin and Evolution of a Worldview*. Boulder, CO: Westview Press.

Smith, Andrew F. 2002. *Peanuts: The Illustrious History of the Goober Pea*. Chicago: University of Illinois Press.

Smith, Monica L. 2007. Inconspicuous Consumption: Non-Display Goods and Identity Formation. *Journal of Archaeological Method and Theory* 14: 412–438.

Southern Poverty Law Center. 2011. *Ku Klux Klan: A History of Racism and Violence*. Montgomery, AL: The Southern Poverty Law Center.

Springate, Megan E., and Amy Raes. 2013. The Power of Choice: Reflections of Economic Ability, Status, and Ethnicity in the Foodways of a Free African American Family in Northwestern New Jersey. *Northeast Historical Archaeology* 42: 6–28.

Stack, Carol B. 2008. *All Our Kin: Strategies for Survival in a Black Community*. New York: Basic Books.

Thomason, Eric J. 2002. A Place Forgotten: Lower Howard's Creek, Kentucky as an Example of Changing Industrial and Consumer Landscapes, the John and Rachel Martin House (Site 15CK478). Paper presented at the 59th Annual Southeastern Archaeological Conference, Biloxi, Mississippi, November 6–9.

Tillery, Alvin B., Jr. 2018. *CSDD & 23AndMe Race and Genomics Survey*. Center for the Study of Diversity and Democracy, Weinberg College of Arts & Sciences, Northwestern University. Accessed October 16, 2020. https://csdd.northwestern.edu/research/csdd-23andme-race-and-genomics-survey-2018.html.

Township of Westampton, New Jersey. 2015. Timbuctoo Village. Accessed June 13, 2019. https://www.westamptonnj.gov/about/pages/timbuctoo-village.

Turton, Catherine. 1999. *Timbuctoo: Burlington County, New Jersey*. Philadelphia: National Park Service.

United States Department of Agriculture. 2011. *Custom Soil Resource Report for Burlington County, New Jersey: Timbuctoo Area*. Natural Resources Conservation Service, United States Department of Agriculture. Web Soil Survey. http://websoilsurvey.nrcs.usda.gov/app/WebSoilSurvey.aspx.

Veblen, Thorstein. 1899. *Theory of the Leisure Class: An Economic Study of Institutions*. New York: MacMillan.

Vera Institute of Justice. 2019. *Incarceration Trends in New Jersey*. Brooklyn, New York: Vera Institute of Justice.

Wall, Diana D. 1999. Examining Gender, Class and Ethnicity in Nineteenth-Century New York City. *Historical Archaeology* 33(1): 102–117.

Wall, Diana Di Zerega. 1991. Sacred Dinners and Secular Teas: Constructing Domesticity in Mid-19th-Century New York. *Historical Archaeology* 25(4): 69–81.

Weik, Terrance M. 2012. *The Archaeology of Antislavery Resistance*. Gainesville: University Press of Florida.

Weston, Guy. 2018. New Jersey: A State Divided on Freedom. *Journal of the Afro-African Historical and Genealogical Society* 34: 2–3.

Weyeneth, Robert R. 2005. The Architecture of Racial Segregation: The Challenges of Preserving the Problematical Past. *Public Historian* 27(4): 11–44.

Wieczorek, Scott, and Susan D. Grzybowski. 2008. *Phase IB Archaeological Investigation Saddler's Run Watershed Restoration: Haddon Township, Camden County, New Jersey, Site Report.* Morristown, NJ: Louis Berger Group.

Wilkie, Laurie A. 2000. *Creating Freedom: Material Culture and African American Identity at Oakley Plantation, Louisiana, 1840–1950.* Baton Rouge: Louisiana State University Press.

Wilkie, Laurie A., and Paul Farnsworth. 2011. Living Not So Quietly, Not So on the Edge of Things: A Twentieth Century Bahamian Household. In *The Materiality of Freedom: Archaeologies of Postemancipation Life,* edited by Jodi A. Barnes, 58–68. Columbia: University of South Carolina.

Wood, Margaret C. 2002. "Fighting for Our Homes": An Archaeology of Women's Domestic Labor and Social Change in a Working-Class Coal-Mining Community 1900–1930. PhD diss., Syracuse University, Syracuse, NY.

Wright, Giles R. 1989. *Afro-Americans in New Jersey: A Short Story.* Trenton: New Jersey Historical Commission.

Wurst, LouAnn, and Robert Fitts, eds. 1999. Confronting Class. *Historical Archaeology* 33(1).

Wurst, LouAnn, and Randall H. McGuire. 1999. Immaculate Consumption: A Critique of the "Shop till you Drop" School of Human Behavior. *International Journal of Historical Archaeology* 3(3) 191–199.

Yang, Mimi. 2018. Trumpism: A Disfigured Americanism. *Palgrave Communications* 4:117.

Yentsch, Anne E. 1994. *A Chesapeake Family and Their Slaves: A Study in Historical Archaeology.* Cambridge: Cambridge University Press.

INDEX

The letters *t* and *i* refer to tables and illustrations.

Christopher P. Barton is assistant professor of archaeology at Francis Marion University. He is interested in the archaeology of race and the use of archaeology as a medium for social activism. He is the coauthor of *Historical Racialized Toys in the United States* (with Kyle Somerville) and the editor of editor of *Trowels in the Trenches: Archaeology as Social Activism*. He lives in Myrtle Beach, SC with his wife, son, and dogs.